Comfort My People

Christian counselling
– a lay challenge –

Foreword by Dr David A. Seamands

Isaac and Shirley Lim

Dear Ann

May God continue to bless you and use you as His agent of comfort and joy. Blessings!

Sovereign World

Isaak Lim

Nashville
16 Oct. '98.

Sovereign World Ltd
PO Box 777
Tonbridge
Kent TN11 9XT
England

Singapore Edition:
First published by Methodist Book Room, Singapore, 1988
    ISBN 981–00–0667–7 (paperback)
    ISBN 981–00–0740–X (hardcover)

International Edition:
Sovereign World International 1993
    ISBN 1 85240 105 2

Typeset by CRB (Drayton) Typesetting Services, Norwich
Printed in England by Clays Ltd, St Ives plc

To our beloved children,
Gloria and Charis,
who we know will carry on
God's message of love in their own time.
They have been God's special gifts to us.
We thank God each day for them.

Contents

Acknowledgements

The writing of this book has been a very enriching experience for us. We have written and revised this manuscript about a dozen times before printing it in this form. In spite of the many revisions, we notice glaring omissions and recognise the limitations of our work. Yet we feel a deep compulsion to share the experiences that we have had in the ministry of comfort with the hope that many will be blessed.

We have spent about three years snatching time here and there from our very busy schedule to write this book. We want to first of all give thanks to God for the burden He has placed in our hearts for a ministry of care and comfort. As we have ourselves experienced His comfort, we are compelled to share the same with others. To Him we give all the glory and praise.

We also would like to give thanks to God for the many Christians we know who love the Lord and who have stood amidst trials to reach out to others, regardless of rank or status. They have brought the joy of the Lord to others and have affirmed to many the beauty and power of God's love and grace.

We would like to take this opportunity to acknowledge with thanks the many members of our Church, who have worked alongside us, contributing in different ways to the ministries of nurture, evangelism, mission and outreach.

Their dedication to these ministries have inspired us and we praise God for them. We thank God for a rising concern for personal ministries at the level of lay Christians and know that God is doing a great work in awakening in our spirits a renewed verve for sharing, caring and teaching in the power of the Holy Spirit.

We praise God for loving parishioners. They have made our ministry a challenging one. As we have expressed our love for them, they have in many ways expressed their love for us. They have grown to trust us and have allowed us entry into the privacy of their joys and pains. It has been through these many encounters with parishioners that we have gained insights to human behaviour and skills in the ministry of counselling and care.

We owe a special depth of gratitude to our friends and parishioners who have encouraged us to write this book. We are also grateful for the love and encouragement of those whose lives have touched ours in a personal way. We would like to thank each one of them by name, but the list would be unending.

We cannot adequately express our gratitude to Prof. and Mrs David A. Seamands for their friendship and encouragement in the writing of this book. Prof. Seamands took valuable time from his hectic schedule to read the manuscript, make his comments and write the foreword. We would also like to acknowledge with thanks the contributions of Dr John Haggai, Dr John Gallock, and Bishop Emerito P. Nacpil who not only read the manuscript but also took time to share their invaluable comments. Mr Desmond Pereira must also be thanked for valuable time spent in assisting us in the editing stages of this book. We value their friendship and interest in this project.

We have used the Bible quite extensively in this book, and we want to acknowledge with thanks the Lockman Foundation for their generosity in allowing us permission to quote from the New American Standard Version.

Acknowledgements

Finally, we want to thank God for you. We pray that God will bless you through the pages of this book and may you be a blessing to many others.

God bless and keep you.

Isaac Lim and Shirley Lim

Foreword

With the rapid rise of personal and relational problems it has become increasingly clear there are simply not enough professionally trained counsellors to meet the need. Many of us have learned the hard way the perils of trying to fill people's needs when we are depleted or empty from over-loaded schedules. Like our Lord himself, drained from constant contact with the crowds, we too say that strength has gone out of us.

This is what happened to Isaac and Shirley Lim in the explosive growth of their ministry at Wesley Methodist Church, Singapore. Drawn by Isaac's Spirit-anointed preaching, a wide range of church sponsored services and joyous vitality of music and worship, people began seeking help for their problems – emotional, spiritual and marital. Soon the Lims found themselves literally forced into a counselling ministry which reached far beyond the boundaries of their own parish. Most exciting of all they discovered, as I had when a missionary in India and a pastor in America *that a counselling ministry can become a major part of the church's evangelistic outreach in winning non-Christians to Christ!*

With divine discernment and direction they wisely avoided the major pitfall of counselling – one-to-one individualized counselling which becomes a side eddy separated from the main stream of the body-life of the church.

Through a careful plan of counsellor training for those who possessed the 'gifts and graces' for this ministry they now have an incredible number of laypersons on the team. But they didn't stop there. The whole ministry of care, comfort and counselling has been woven into the life of the church through a network of small groups and prayer partners. During our two week stay in Singapore I was again and again introduced to men and women who said they 'worked at Wesley', or were 'on the team'. Thinking in American terms of a paid church staff I was amazed and thrilled to discover they were volunteers who regularly gave a scheduled time for this ministry. Best of all they looked at themselves as an important part of the life of the church.

All this means that this book is not some theory of lay counselling and group dynamics which the Lims have gotten out of textbooks and challenge us to follow. It is real, and describes what is now taking place in a local church. So regardless of your theories of counselling it deserves your careful reading. It is biblical, psychologically sound, and puts into everyday practice the amazing power of a church determined to be literally a caring community of believers. I commend it to you and intend to use some of its suggestions in my own courses.

Dr David A. Seamands
Professor of Pastoral Ministries
Asbury Theological Seminary

Chapter 1

Comfort My People

A Crying Need

The cry for help is all around us. Behind smiling faces, looks of confidence, facades of success, lie aching hearts, yearning for some release. Can help be found?

Some time ago, a man walked into my (Isaac's) office. Young, rugged, intelligent and successful. He had called the same afternoon to say that he was coming. Within minutes of his call, he arrived. Peter was a vibrant person, but that day he looked different. He began to quiver as he spoke, his voice choking with emotion. 'Pastor,' he quietly said, 'my physician has just told me that I may be suffering from throat cancer. I've not spoken to my wife or children about it yet but I thought I'll talk to you first before breaking the news to them. Pastor, I've come to ask you to pray with me.'

I took time to listen to him, to empathize with his fears and minister to him. I wanted him to know that we cared, that God cared, and that Jesus stood with him in the midst of his despair. He wept, as he shared his fears, his anxieties, his apprehensions, and his dilemma. He thought of his wife, his children, their future, his future. I held his clammy hands and together we prayed. We cried unto the Lord for His touch of mercy and asked that His hand be upon Peter in his situation.

A week later, I received a call from him. 'Pastor,' he said, 'I've just received news from my doctor. He says that I'm all right. Tests have shown that there's nothing wrong with me. Pastor, I just want you to know how much I appreciate your willingness to counsel with me. When I needed somebody to talk to, you were there.'

There are people all over in similar situations. They need someone who can provide that listening ear; someone who would try to understand; someone who would hold them by the hand and say, 'I care'. In this world of stress and strain, you can be that someone whom God can use to bring comfort, counsel, help, and support for someone in need.

Samantha looked composed and elegant in her floral dress. There were traces of weariness in her eyes but she greeted me very warmly. I (Shirley) was told earlier by her friend who had made the appointment for her to see me that she had recently lost two of her children in two months. She had also attempted suicide twice after their death. As all three of us sat down to talk, she recounted how her Christian friends supported her all through the period of her bereavement. They took turns to sit with her, bringing her out shopping, to the hairdresser's and to Christian meetings.

As I listened to her relate the events of her children's death and of how she had felt as she watched them die one after the other in almost the same way, I could empathize with the numbing pain she must have gone through. I commented that it must have been a very painful experience and asked her how she found the strength to cope so well so far. She told me how her Christian friends had prayed for her, and, though she was not a Christian, she had since her days in a Christian school been very open to the gospel. She shared with me the uplifting effect of the prayers of her friends who visited her regularly. While even some of her relatives avoided her and wondered if she were under the influence of some 'ill-luck' or 'evil', the love of her Christian friends reflected to her the reality of Christ's love. Things were well for a while, and then she began to have suicidal thoughts again and had a gripping desire to join her children by taking her own life. She even wanted to die the same way they did. She knew that since she felt the touch of Christ's love, she should not entertain such thoughts, but she said that they came involuntarily and she could not control herself.

As we conferred together, we began to discover that she had a deep sense of guilt over the children's death. She felt she had never been a good mother as she had been busy managing a large business concern and also had a very busy social life. As we prayed over her deep sense of guilt, she realised that the Lord Jesus had taken her guilt and her sin and nailed them on the Cross and that she didn't need to pay the price. The Holy Spirit confirmed the truth of Christ's cleansing power in her experience and she was released from her anguish. She received a deep peace and called some weeks later to say that she had strength to resume her work and to begin to live again. Samantha thanked us for giving her the much needed support and we gave thanks to God.

A Challenge to All

There is a growing conviction that the responsibility of counselling is no longer the monopoly of the pastor or the professional counsellor but the responsibility of all Christians, both clergy and lay. We are convinced that the biblical imperative for counselling is not directed at the professionals alone, but at all of God's children who desire to share the love of God with others.

In our time and age, the complexities of modern living have taken their toll on many people, both Christian and non-Christian. Stress-related ailments and disorders are rampant and many people just cannot cope with their lives. In a recent survey carried out by an international labour organisation, we are told that the stresses and strains in modern industrial life result in serious mental or emotional disorders in one out of every four workers. Some of the reasons given include high expectations at work, close supervision, impersonal attitudes among the management, high noise level, etc. This is reported as one of the world's most serious social and health problems.

The hustle and bustle of modern living is so pervasive a force in so many parts of the world that people are swept off their feet into the perennial rush. There is little time for self, little time for family, little time for friends and little time for God. Not only are there competing demands and pressures on all sides but change and instability prevail.

In a time of economic instability, a further pressure is added. Economic changes threaten to rock the very foundations of personal life. Because there is little time to establish close ties and meaningful relationships, personal problems take on a greater magnitude than ever before. Satan strikes at the very heart of this situation to wreak destruction and despair in many a life.

It is against this backdrop that many persons, including Christians, find themselves caught in an ever-tightening web of conflicting demands and competing pressures from all sides. Some soon find themselves tied up in some nasty psychological knots and unable to draw loose. Often, prolonged pressure and emotional stress have left many battered and bruised. Is there a comfort and release?

The age-old message is that Jesus can set us free. Not only free from the crippling psychological traps that bind us but also free to live out the abundant life that He has promised us in Scripture in the book of John. John 10:10 records the assurance Jesus gives to us that, *'The thief comes only to steal, and kill, and destroy; I came that they might have life, and might have it abundantly.'* Satan has indeed stolen a great deal from us and has destroyed the lives of many people trapped in depression, guilt, grief, fear and anxiety. Many destroy themselves and their loved ones because life has become purposeless and threatening. The Christian who has tasted the goodness of the Lord is Satan's chief target. Haven't we observed that the fruit of the Spirit, that is, love, joy, peace, patience, kindness, goodness, faithfulness, gentleness and self-control (Galatians 5:22) has often been replaced by hatred, sadness, anxiety, impatience, unkindness, wickedness, faithlessness, anger and aggression? How can we help the individual Christian to live a Spirit-filled life that manifests the fruit of the Spirit, and not be overwhelmed by the human tendencies that are the antithesis of the life Christ meant us to have? We believe that this is a question that involves not only the individual Christian but the whole Church as the Body of Christ. As the fabric of social life changes, the texture of the Church community must also be strengthened as a response to resulting personal needs.

The Church's Role

The Church today needs to address directly the rising need for psychological, emotional and spiritual support especially in places where physical needs have largely been adequately met. The social masks of cordiality and remoteness need not always be worn in the gatherings of saints. We should concentrate instead on building up and upholding basic principles of love and faith and mutual trust in bonds that cannot be broken. These bonds can only be established when real feelings and experiences are shared and treasured. The double blessing of having Christian friends to turn to in times of need as well as to minister to in times of well-being is the rich heritage of the Christian.

A time of crisis is often a time when values are reassessed. When a person is down and out, he can be helped by caring Christians to appropriate the teachings and promises of Christ. As he responds to the counsel and comfort offered he experiences a free flow of God's grace. Those who support and identify with him are also blessed, as they become a part of that means of grace.

The amazing grace of our Lord Jesus Christ is available for all – even the least among us. The fullness of the Gospel of Christ lies in its relevance to all men in all situations. In fact Scripture reminds us specifically in Matthew 25 of the importance of ministering to the least amongst us. This reminder is a particularly strong one. It is therefore imperative for the Christian personally, and the Christian Church collectively, to work out the relevance of the Gospel of Christ to the human situation in this day and age.

This is a season of spiritual harvest for many nations of the world. Persons caught up in the web of social, emotional and psychological entanglement look for an answer to their situation. They are not looking for a temporary, external consolation because they have seen how transient prosperity and materialism can be. What is sought after is an enduring, lasting peace, which brings inner wholeness and well-being. This we know only Jesus can give.

For those of us who love Jesus, this is the season of ministry. There are many who have been buffeted by the storms of life and are badly bruised, damaged and broken within. They are ready to receive the healing balm of our Lord Jesus.

Our church, like many other churches, has been looked at as a place of ministry for many years now. We have seen the mighty hand of the Lord at work not only in the numerical growth of the church but also in the strengthening and transforming of lives. With rapid growth, we have inevitably seen the expansion of person-to-person ministries. Family members have been brought to church for ministry; friends and colleagues have come; new acquaintances, even strangers have been invited to see if Jesus could be the answer to their predicaments. It is not unusual each week to find sixty or seventy persons visiting the church for the first time. Many have come because someone has told them that they have found Christ meeting their needs through the ministry of the church.

We Can Help

'Can you help me?' a distressed lady poured out her woes. 'I don't know what has come over me. Since I discovered last month that my husband has another woman, I've been on the verge of suicide several times. I don't really want to die!' added the pretty, well-dressed lady. 'I have a lovely son and two beautiful daughters – but you know, there are times when I feel so low that I have even tried strangling myself! ... Please help me,' she sobbed.

We feel it is good to be able to say affirmatively, 'We can help, yet not us but Christ.' By the grace of God, it has been possible to help many others like her during a period of crisis, and many have today not only found a new life in Christ but have been able to help others also. Some came with problems of demon-possession, others had gripping fears and hallucinations; still others were depressed and without hope; even children as young as four years of age were brought because of emotional problems.

God's Word and the ministry of the Holy Spirit are relevant to all human needs. To see lives transformed is in itself a joyful experience. It is difficult to say in our context whether it is because of the ministry of prayer, care and counselling that the church has grown, or whether it is because of church growth that the ministry of care and counselling has become prominent. The fact however remains that as a result of rapid church growth, there has been an accompanying conviction of the need to provide personal ministry in the area of prayer, care and counselling.

We believe that the Church must provide an avenue

where true spirituality can be expressed. The acquisition of biblical and theological knowledge alone is insufficient. Theology must be practical if it is to be alive. Theology must be related to the daily encounters of God's people. Theology must not remain only in the realm of the intellect, it must spur God-centred Christians into dynamic action that will bring solace and healing to suffering people. Christians have been called to do just that.

A Call to Comfort

In Isaiah 40:1, the word of God comes to Isaiah saying, *'Comfort, O comfort My people.'* It came at a time when the people needed to hear words of comfort. The prophet was to go and speak kindly to Jerusalem. He was to bring words of hope and encouragement to a defeated and lost nation. God was to act, and he would bring about renewal in the lives of His people. In verse 31 of the same chapter, Isaiah is to bring these words of encouragement – *'those who wait for the Lord will gain new strength; they will mount up with wings like eagles, they will run and not get tired, they will walk and not become weary.'*

Isaiah's call to bring comfort to a needy people is also our call for today. The Lord's strength is available for the distressed, the harassed, and the disturbed. The kind of comfort given to the troubled is not a comfort that is temporary or ordinary but a comfort that enables us to gain a 'new strength' – a kind of strength we've never had before. This strength is supernatural. It is a strength that enables us to 'mount up with wings as eagles'; it is the strength that enables us to soar above problems and not be defeated by the natural attrition of life's toils; it is a strength that can come only from God. There is a call for those of us who love the Lord not only to experience continually God's comfort in this way but also to minister His love and comfort to those who are without them.

Agents of Comfort

It is without a doubt that God has called us to be agents of His comfort. The imperative to Isaiah and to us is *'to comfort all who mourn ... giving them a garland instead of ashes ... the oil of gladness instead of mourning, the mantle of praise instead of a spirit of fainting'* (Isaiah 61:2–3) so that God may be glorified.

The imperative for us is to comfort God's people. In a sense, God's people is the world. It is because He loved the world that He gave His only Son so that whoever believes in Him should not perish but have eternal life. The Gospel of Christ is a gospel of hope and comfort. This is the world that is in need of hope and comfort. He has called us to be bearers of His comfort to His people.

The more the Christian draws near to Christ, the more he experiences the love of God. The more the Christian draws near to Christ, the greater will be the call to reach out in loving personal ministry to others. The Christian will experience joy in the ministry of service and counselling, when his involvement is a response to God's call. As the Christian finds fulfilment in Christ, he appropriates for himself the identity of a child of God. As such he experiences the reality of the comfort of Christ, and is able and constrained by the love of Christ to help others also. The comforted counsellor is a Christian who has himself experienced the reality of God's comfort through some personal struggles along life's journey. It is not uncommon to see even new Christians who have experienced the touch of God's comfort receiving a strong call to give true encouragement to others, particularly those going through similar afflictions.

Victor and Jean were friends of a member of our church. They were brought to the church for counselling as their marriage relationship was strained and they had violent fights frequently. Victor was an alcoholic and Jean was an idealist. Though they loved one another and wanted to remain married for the sake of the children, they would end up sometimes brutally hurting one another in their fury. It seemed a rather hopeless situation when Jean became mentally distressed and was often warded for intensive medical care. One day Victor heard of the love of Jesus. Coming to Christ in confession and repentance, he was freed not only from alcoholism and chain-smoking but was able to help Jean back to health. We observed in Victor a change in his person as he accepted Jesus and grew in his faith. There was a new and compelling desire to reach out and help others. He brought some of his friends with marital problems for help and would go out of his way to listen to his friends, especially those who were hurting or in distress. He asked us if it was all right for him to share with others and help them even though he was then only a very new Christian. We could see how genuinely he wanted to comfort others, having been himself comforted in his predicament by the God Who loves and comforts.

Comforted to Comfort

Those of us who have experienced the comfort of Christ in our afflictions know that it is a comfort that builds us up. God has often allowed trials, tribulations and suffering to come our way so that we may be raised to the stature of Christ through His enabling. As we go through furnaces of difficulty in our lives, we become refined as we learn to trust in God's comforting presence. We will not be consumed, as we trust in His grace and receive His comfort. Just as Shadrach, Meshach and Abednego (Daniel 3) experienced a deliverance from the fury of the furnace, so too will we be given every grace and comfort to brave life's trials. Very often we have seen in tangible ways how God brings His people through rough times in life so that they may, like Job, be refined in character and *'come forth as gold'* (Job 23:10). It is therefore important to realise that involving ourselves in a ministry of comfort to others does not mean that we are ourselves free from problems altogether. We often hear our members say, 'As you know, I still have a few problems I've not been able to resolve, and I guess they can't be for some time to come, but I do feel a great urge to do my bit to help others and touch their lives with Christ's love. What should I do?'

We have thought through this question along with our friends and members and we are often touched by the genuineness of many who want to spread the love of Christ by touching other lives. We believe that this desire comes from God as it is in accordance with His general will for our lives. We need however to seek God's specific direction and await His time in deciding on the nature and extent of our involvement. There will be the initial apprehensions and hesitations but if it is a call from the Lord in specific areas of ministry, we will also receive the empowerment and ability. We believe that this is the season of ministry when God is raising our awareness of human need. He is also making His resources available to us to meet these needs in ways we have perhaps not experienced before.

Allow us at this point to share with you a personal calling. We have been actively involved in the ministry of the Church together for close to twenty years now. In the first ten years or so, God gave us a wonderful evangelical fervour in our ministry together. We loved God dearly and gave our lives willingly to serve Him. It has always been an engaging and rewarding ministry for us, going through thick and thin together. It was therefore with great surprise that we felt at one point of our lives that God was calling us to a greater commitment in a fuller ministry. Isaac was then the associate pastor of the largest Methodist Church in Singapore and Shirley was then teaching full-time, on top of being mother to a seven-year old and a pastor's wife in a growing church. 'Haven't we already been stretched to capacity in our service and gone flat out for you, Lord?' we heard ourselves asking God. 'How is it that You seem to be telling us about fuller service?' We soon received the answer to our questions.

It was the time just before the birth of our second child Charis. We had been busy doing a lot of the routine as we served the Lord, and after our first child turned six we thought it was time to have another child. It was at this time that we entered into a special phase in our spiritual lives when we felt close to the Lord in a special way. We seemed to be able to hear quite clearly what He was saying to us specifically. We knew the Lord would bless us with a baby boy even before he was born. We were led to call him 'Charis' which is a Greek word meaning 'grace' or 'gift from God'. It was a time of spiritual renewal for us as we were blessed with the gift of tongues for the purpose of a prayer ministry.

When Charis was born, he surprised even the doctors as he weighed only about 3 pounds and 13 ounces. He was healthy and grew rapidly. When he was three months old, however, he contracted a viral infection that resulted in a high and persistent fever for three days and three nights. The doctors suspected meningitis or even worse, encephalitis, which are infections of the outer and inner brain. We prayed for healing and the Lord assured us of healing for our child, and gave us peace. Nothing could be done medically for our child, we were told, and we should just pray. On the third night of Charis' illness, Shirley was led to request that he be removed from the machines and drip that he was attached to. Almost instantaneously, Charis' fever subsided and in less than six hours, he was completely healed and was able to be bottle-fed. He was quickly discharged from the hospital within hours. Our child's healing was one of the first miraculous healings we've witnessed as we prayed in the Name of Jesus and in His love.

A whole new dimension was added to our ministry. We learnt from this experience what it meant to receive God's comfort in the face of hopelessness and anguish. We knew then what God meant when we heard His call to us to fuller commitment. It was a call to boldly believe in God as the one who is almighty and able to do the impossible. We realised what it meant to enlarge our experiential concept of God and to believe in a supernatural God who cares enough for us to intervene and meet our needs in our day to day living and ministry.

As God continues to demonstrate His love and care for us and for so many of our friends and members, we feel led to share His goodness and work with others in this time and age. As the social fabric of modern living presents its imposing patterns of independent living and self-reliance, a return to the biblical heritage of togetherness and dependence on God is a message we've been called to share. We trust that as we come just as we are in sincere submission to our Master, He will be able to use us to touch others with His comfort. In ourselves, we are certainly never fully equipped to be of much help to others but we are called to be obedient to His directives of caring for the least amongst us, as Christ reminds us that when we minister comfort to those in need we are in fact ministering to Him.

A Gift of Comfort

The theme of comfort runs through the Bible. The fact that our God is a God of comfort is evident from Genesis to Revelation. We cannot read Scripture without noticing the comforting presence of God in the varied encounters of life. The compassion of God reaches out to suffering people and is well illustrated in the book of Isaiah from where the title of our book is taken (Isaiah 40:1).

The comfort of God always brings joy to the recipient of comfort. Isaiah says in 49:13, *'Shout for joy, O heavens! And rejoice, O earth! Break forth into joyful shouting, O mountains! For the Lord has comforted His people, and will have compassion on His afflicted.'* When the Lord comforts His people, the outcome of that comfort will be a wonderful experience of joy.

In the very run of life when comfort is needed, we must recognise that God alone is the ultimate source of all comfort. In Isaiah 51:12 He says, *'I, even I, am He who comforts you.'* Although men are used by God as channels of His comfort, and we need to be worthy channels of His comfort, the fact remains that God is the one who finally brings calm and peace to our souls.

It is interesting to note the mother image that is given to God as the Comforter. In Isaiah 66:13 God says, *'As one whom his mother comforts, so I will comfort you.'* There is always a special relationship between a mother and a child. The mother instinct is always to protect her children and bring words of support and encouragement to lift the spirit of a defeated child. God is like that. He comes to us like a mother, embraces us with His arms of love, tells us that He loves us and reminds us that everything will be all right because He is in complete control.

The message of the Gospel of Christ is that there is a balm to soothe all manner of distress – physical, mental, emotional and spiritual. Jesus, in His death for us on the cross, has redeemed us from sin and released us from all forms of bondage. When we believe in Christ's blood as an atonement of our sins, we need also to believe that He can also set us free from the obsessive effects of fears, anxieties, guilt and depression. As the American folk hymn goes,

> 'There is a balm in Gilead, to make the wounded
>   whole;
> There is a balm in Gilead, to heal the sin-sick soul.
> Sometimes I feel discouraged,
> And think my work's in vain,
> But then the Holy Spirit
> Revives my soul again
> There is a balm in Gilead, to make the wounded
>   whole:
> There is a balm in Gilead, to heal the sin-sick soul.'

Is it not wonderful to know that Jesus gives us comfort in our distress?

A lovely Christian lady related her experience of comfort from our Lord Jesus. She recalled how her husband committed suicide and how during the last days of his life he had in his deranged state of mind heaped blame and abuse on her. Her spirit was deeply hurt and broken, and after his death she sought psychiatric help. Even whilst sedated, she related dreams and nightmares that disturbed her. She began to twitch and very often went into tantrums and fits of fear. Her loved ones were most supportive, but when she closed her eyes in sleep, the inner horrors plagued her. How tremendous therefore it was for her when Jesus' comfort was ministered and she received the gift of His comforting presence. She explained how she dreamt one night of the sensation of a comforting light, a brightness that was not glaring. There was no darkness because of the light. A figure she thought to be that of Jesus approached her and she could feel the strength of the hands of Jesus as they rested upon her head. Since her vision, she had a beautiful image of comfort in her mind that replaced the horrors of her past. Occasionally, she says, the fears come back especially when she is stressed or over-tired, but now she has recourse to Jesus' presence deep within her soul. Jesus can comfort us in a deep and personal way.

Christian Counselling Revisited

Christian counselling has been practised since the days of the early Church. Paul exhorts his fellow Christians with these words, '*And we urge you, brethren, admonish the unruly, encourage the faint-hearted, help the weak, be patient with all men*' (1 Thessalonians 5:14).

In recent times, with the proliferation of systematic studies and specialisations in the areas of secular as well as Christian counselling, differing schools of thought and approaches generate controversy and some degree of cloudiness and confusion in the thinking of laypersons. Are the Noutheticists right in saying that the Bible is the one authority in counselling persons with needs as it has the answer to all problems of the human predicament? Or are some of the secular psychologists, counsellors and psychiatrists right to say that counselling should best be left to the experts?

These waves of advancement in knowledge and know-how in pastoral counselling and care, together with the accompanying controversy, have in some quarters raised levels of awareness of the need and impact of counselling. But at the same time, they have also, to a considerable degree, left the Christian to seek security in non-involvement, for fear of treading on delicate ground.

This book does not attempt to discuss such controversies related to the area of counselling. The approach adopted is eclectic, and we hope to move away from adherence to any one theoretical stand. We shall attempt to discuss the concept of counselling as laid down in Scripture and to relate that to the work of the Holy Spirit in the life of the Church today. A biblical framework for the ministry of counselling within the local church will be set up and the scriptural guidelines for effective ministry will be laid down. In all this it is hoped that the central place of Christ in Christian counselling will be emphasized, and the work and the power of the Holy Spirit be revealed, shared and honoured. Through this shared experience, we hope to challenge and encourage Christians in the ministry of counselling so that many lives may be touched to receive the Grace of our Lord Jesus Christ.

As God has blessed and used us, we feel led to articulate here some of the practical implications of an integrative approach that we have attempted to work out in leading our church to stand as a corporate witness of God's love, and to offer to all a ministry of Christ's love.

We have ourselves been so deeply touched by the reality of Christ's love through our contacts with our members that we want to share the fresh meanings we've discovered in the building up of a ministry of love and care within the assembly of God's House. We have seen the empowerment of the Holy Spirit in the lives of many, including our own, in the last ten years as we learn what it means to touch and be touched by others in a ministry of comfort and caring in Jesus' Name.

In our experience, the more we believed in reaching out and comforting others, the more comfort and empowerment we received to equip us for further work. We saw the fulfilling of scriptural truths unfolding, such as the drawing together of God's people in one unity and one love as expressed in Philippians 2:2.

The sense of unity is real as we fight many of life's battles together. The griefs of bereavement, the hurts of abandonment, the torments of rejection, the anguish of ailments and the distress of failure are just some of the shared experiences. This sense of togetherness is one that is full of hope and encouragement as we confirm the reality of God's grace amongst us. How can we not be strengthened in heart and mind and soul when collective prayers are answered and grace and peace received? Even when God's answer to us was 'no', there has been grace and peace in abundance. We will never forget those among us who died of cancer, of the days of advancing pain and prayers, and of how God gave them such peace and grace that, with their weakening breaths, they encouraged us instead with exhortations of joy in Christ. While we rejoice at physical healing that sometimes takes place as a result of prayer, inner spiritual healing is equally heartwarming. United in a victory in Christ, who can break the ties that bind us in Christian love? Having laughed together, rejoiced together, agonised together and wept together, the Church for many of us is a vital part of our existence as our lives touch and intertwine.

One dear sister who was terminally ill with cancer said this to us, 'When I first realised I had a malignant cancer, I felt numb all over. But now I wake up each morning with a great sense of a peace that passes all understanding at being able to see a new day. I'd like you to share this with others that there is such a thing as peace and joy in suffering.' This is what we hope to share in this book.

As we minister and are ministered to within the Body of Christ in this way, as life touches life at significant and real junctures of life's journey, it becomes imperative for us to protest against the impression of the church as a place where people are expected to simply look their best however beaten up they may feel within. It has really been good to see that God has given to many the grace to open up and share their pains and their battles as well as their joys with others, so that comfort and upliftment are received and each is covered with his brother's love.

The Church's Witness

We are convinced that the larger the church, the stronger the personal ministries must be. Personal ministries take place within the larger framework of the Christ-centred community. There is a need for anointed worship, teaching, and preaching. These corporate experiences are important means of grace. Our members frequently bring in friends and visitors to share in our worship experiences. Many testify to a heart-warming experience of God's comforting presence just by sitting quietly in the pews. Others have received special ministry at Holy Communion Services as they experience a touch of God's love and grace. Our altars are stained over the years with tears of repentance and the joy of forgiveness and release.

How can this be explained except that a mighty flow of the Spirit has been experienced? The gentle breeze of God's Spirit breaks down barriers deep in our souls and releases us to a new freedom to love and to live for Him by loving others. Expressions of God's touch on individual lives differ but what is common is the emergence of a conviction among many who have received a special portion of God's love that they would like to share it with others.

As individual members seek to express their personal response to God's love, we can join hands to reach out to others. We can build a supportive network to comfort and care for those amongst us or those who come to us with needs, however large or small. Together it is possible for us to build an atmosphere of acceptance, love and trust in the Name of Jesus. It is so easy for any church or institution to be a cold and impersonal place where members dare not reveal any trace of hurt or defeat or confusion for fear of censure or even condemnation. The Church must instead be a place where members and others may come just as they are and in honesty and openness find comfort and practical meaning in Christ's love. For the repentant, the Church is a haven of blessing and a place of peace.

Hence, Christian counselling, as we see it, is not only relevant to the care of the highly distressed, but is also a practice that edifies the church as a whole as members engage meaningfully in mutual ministry and uphold one another in fervent prayer.

A Lay Challenge

Why do we say that Christian counselling is a lay challenge? Why shouldn't we leave Christian counselling to the professionals such as specially trained pastors and professional counsellors? We believe that many specialists and professionals in counselling have been and will continue to be used by God mightily in the ministry to suffering persons. However, their roles are specialised and their time and influence as individuals must needs be limited. Just as professional counsellors, pastors and persons in the helping professions have a specific role to play in the counselling ministry, so does the laity. The roles of professional personnel in counselling are more established

and therefore more explicit. The role of the laity, however, has not been so clearly defined. Yet there has been a
definite call to the laity to minister God's love and therefore a responsibility to articulate more clearly a challenge
to respond to that call. We believe that unless the laity,
the entire body of Christ, take on conscientiously and
deliberately their roles in the ministry to hurting persons
as in the days of the early Church, many opportunities for
the spreading of God's love and grace will be gone and
lost forever. The early Christians were ministering in the
way that their master, Jesus, did, without apology for
their lack of expertise or learning. After all, the great
Master Himself was by their side, available for consulta-
tion at all times and giving the divine unction and authority.

We believe that today our great Master is still and ever
will be by our side to give that unction and authority as He
calls us to minister like He did to persons who were
distressed, unhappy and lost. Scripture abounds in exhortations to us as God's children to love, nurture, encourage, help, rescue, direct, teach and pray for anyone in
need who comes by us. Surely God does not give us a
commission without the empowerment.

The reason why Christian counselling is to us a lay
challenge and a ministry of the entire body of Christ is
because there is a **calling** to fulfil, a **mission** of ministry to
hurting persons, and together with the calling, an
empowerment that is given to the **church** to accomplish
her task in proclaiming **Christ** as the **answer** to all **human
needs**.

A Togetherness

The Church as a whole is involved in the ministry of
Christian counselling. God has blessed some amongst us
with the gift of a person-to-person counselling ministry
and many can receive release, comfort and healing

through counselling sessions. Others amongst us are given the gifts of befriending and care. Small groups within the church provide a domain for mutual ministry and Christian nurture.

We have seen many like Kim who have walked into the church quite disillusioned with life and what it had to offer. With family relationships breaking up and all hope gone, Kim could only turn to Jesus who he had vaguely heard to be a God who cared and loved. Kim found the empathy, love and meaning in life he had been looking for. We had met with Kim for only a few sessions of counselling and prayer before he saw how much Jesus loved him. It took some time before Kim decided to accept Christ as his Lord and Saviour. However, even as he was seeking he had been absorbed into the fellowship of a small caring group.

We have seen repeatedly in our ministry that so many would, like Kim, request baptism after a period of searching within the fellowship of caring Christians. Many would, like Kim, tell us that though they first attended the church services without much expectation, they experienced God's touch in the worship services and the preaching of the Word. When we see persons come week after week for worship services and see their fulfilment in the Lord, we feel blessed. Now in his small caring group, Kim not only receives fellowship but contributes to it as well. Kim has found meaning in life as he finds that Jesus not only meets his personal needs but also enables him to be a means of blessing to others also.

Having had the privilege of seeing God's hand at work in this way in His Church, we have felt led to document a challenge to all who love the Lord to develop together a supportive infrastructure for mutual ministries for outreach through the means of Christian counselling. As God has touched us, we have been blessed by being a part of the channels of blessing to others. We have seen how true fellowship in the Lord within the Body of Christ can transmit the redemptive love of Christ in tangible ways.

Hence, this book is primarily written for the Christian who is sincerely seeking an answer to the question of human need and how God's Word and the Holy Spirit can equip the Church to meet these needs. The purpose is to challenge Christians into an increasingly vital ministry in Christian counselling so that many persons can be uplifted spiritually and find wholeness in Christ. It seeks to share the relevance and power of the full gospel of Christ in the individual Christian on one level, and the collective ministry of the Church at another.

A Call to All

In this book, we hope to share, for the edification of God's people, a vision concerning the concept and work of Christian counselling involving not only full-time members of the pastoral team, but also the dynamic ministry of lay persons, all working in unity as the ministering Body of Christ.

The Christian is called not only to extend a ministry of comfort as an individual but also to be part of the ministry of comfort of the church. The challenge therefore is for Christians to learn what it means to articulate together as a body, working together as a team in a corporate ministry to those in need of comfort. We believe that the call is for lay involvement at two levels: ministering to the needs of others at a personal and individual level, and being part of a church-based team ministry which involves the working together alongside fellow Christians in a shared ministry. Our experience is that there is usually a need for team ministry or Body ministry if we are to minister to the whole person. It has been necessary and possible to build up a supportive network of lay persons working hand-in-hand with full-time professionals such as pastors, psychiatrists, doctors and Christian social workers.

Secondly, the challenge is made to the Church as a whole to mobilize, train, and organise lay persons for the ministry of care and counselling. This is in line with the biblical imperative of a body ministry. The Church should seek to encourage the co-ordinated exercise of various spiritual gifts within the framework of the Church so that many may receive ministry and be blessed. The Church should portray and live up to the goals of a caring and sharing community.

Thirdly, the challenge is also towards a ministry of counselling that has an accountability system. It is not everyone doing his own thing in counselling, but each person submitting to a system which takes its final cues from the Senior Pastor or Elder in charge. We are reminded in Scripture to do things decently and in order and we as Christians need to take this injunction seriously. A system of accountability needs to be developed for effective administration, articulation and follow-up of the holistic counselling ministry.

Fourthly, the challenge is towards a ministry of counselling that is integrative. The counsellor, church organisations, the small groups and the like, have each a responsibility in assisting the counsellee in the process of restoration and wholeness. The various ministries of the church will be called upon to give fellowship support or group support. The goal is towards a common thrust and understanding in the philosophy and practice of counselling so that a cohesive system can be set up. To do this, individual members of the church must take up the challenge to minister as part of the Body. May God ever grant us the grace so to do.

Chapter 2

The Triune Counsellor

The winter of 1977 will remain a memorable year for us. Both of us were enrolled as post-graduate students at the University of Aberdeen. It was on a cold winter morning, when we discovered that we had reached the bottom of our financial resources. Christmas was just round the corner and we knew that the days ahead would be days of faith and adjustments. Gloria, our daughter, was then four years old. What would we do if funds were not forthcoming?

We had left our work and gone in faith for further studies on a very tight or close to impossible budget. We found on Christmas Eve that we had only a few pounds left. There was a need to buy some milk for Gloria and food for the Christmas weekend. We felt anxious but could do nothing except kneel down and pray.

It was in those moments that the caring love of God came to us in the most wonderful way. Through the loving concern of a pastor, who had no idea of our plight, and through persons unknown to us, God met us at our every point of need. That Christmas, God supplied all we needed to make it a memorable one.

Does God care? Yes, He does. He cares for us even when things do not seem to be going our way. The reality of God's love comes to us in many different ways. Was it not Jesus who said,

'...do not be anxious for your life, as to what you shall eat, or what you shall drink; nor for your body, as to what you shall put on. Is not life more than food, and the body than clothing? Look at the birds of the air, they do not sow, neither do they reap, nor gather into barns, and yet your heavenly father feeds them. Are you not worth much more than they?'

(Matthew 6:25–26)

These are words of comfort from a God who really cares. It is apparent from this passage that we are persons of worth and that God loves us and seeks the best for us. He not only responds to us as we pray, but He ministers to us as the Counsellor.

God seeks always to be in contact with His people. He seeks to minister to them through the process of dialogue. The following passages make this apparent:

'"Come now, and let us reason together," Says the LORD, "Though your sins are as scarlet, they will be as white as snow; Though they are red like crimson, they will be like wool."'

(Isaiah 1:18)

'Thus says the LORD who made the earth, the LORD who formed it to establish it, the LORD is His name, "Call to Me, and I will answer you, and I will tell you great and mighty things, which you do not know."'

(Jeremiah 33:2–3)

'Ask, and it shall be given to you; seek, and you shall find; knock, and it shall be opened to you. For every-one who asks receives, and he who seeks finds, and to him who knocks it shall be opened. Or what man is there among you, when his son shall ask him for a loaf, will give him a stone? Or, if he shall ask for a fish, he will not give him a snake will he? If you then, being evil, know how to give good gifts to your

> *children, how much more shall your Father who is in heaven give what is good to those who ask Him!'*
>
> (Matthew 7:7–11)

God wants to give us a listening ear; He wants to talk to us if we would but talk to Him.

The joy of the Christian is to know that we have a Triune God who cares. God in His dealings with us, has demonstrated a compassion, an understanding, and a love to draw us into an experience of comfort, reconciliation and wholeness in Him. A look at the work of God the Father, God the Son, and God the Holy Spirit will show that each is engaged in the ministry of counselling which has led the disturbed, the troubled, the brokenhearted, the lost, the sick, and the dying into a life of hope and renewal.

The example of the Holy Trinity in the ministry of counselling and the commission that God has given to us through Scripture should be sufficient inspiration to spur us on in our ministry of care and counselling.

God the Father

The Bible has countless passages which allude to God as a God of comfort and care. Taking our cue from the Old and New Testaments, we cannot help noticing these passages which talk about God as a compassionate Father who desires to dialogue with us and to lead us in the straight and narrow way. The Bible speaks of a God who counsels His people and communicates with them in the daily events of life. It speaks of a God who gets involved in the affairs of His people, and raises leaders who will bring His word to them in order that they may be delivered from bondage into freedom.

Some of the most touching scenes in the Bible which reveal to us the heart of God are scenes in which the Father approaches His own creation and counsels them. It is touching because it portrays for us a God who in His compassion seeks men and women with the intention of comforting them and bringing them out of their situation of despair into an experience of victory and hope. We see this in God's counselling encounters with Adam (Genesis 3:8–21), Abraham (Genesis 15:1–21), Moses (Exodus 3:1–4:17), Gideon (Judges 7:2–18), and many others.

One interesting encounter however is recorded in 1 Kings 19:1–18 where God takes time to counsel the prophet Elijah and comforts him in his moment of discouragement.

Elijah's Depression

Elijah has just completed a very successful campaign against the prophets of Baal. But he soon receives word that the evil queen, Jezebel, the patron of Baal worship and the wife of the Jewish King Ahab, is out to kill him. Shaken by the news, and fearful of the possible eventuality, he runs for his life to Beersheba. From Beersheba, he takes a day's journey into the wilderness, to Mount Horeb located in the Sinai peninsula.

It should be noted that Mount Carmel, where Elijah defeated the prophets of Baal, and Mount Horeb are about three hundred miles apart. Elijah must have been gripped by intense fear to have travelled such a great distance.

Apparently, Elijah had not expected Jezebel to respond to his victory with such fury. He had just overawed King Ahab and the Baal worshippers by demonstrating the power of God. Convinced that the purity of the Jewish religion needed to be maintained Elijah went ahead with the extermination of the prophets of Baal. This brought upon him the displeasure of Jezebel who purposed in her heart to exterminate him as an act of vengeance.

Elijah had thought that his victory at Mount Carmel would have subdued Jezebel and prepared her to listen with respect to God's prophet and to encourage the king in bringing about religious reforms. But on the contrary, Jezebel swore to avenge the slaughter of her priests through the death of Elijah himself.

One would have thought that a man of Elijah's stature and authority would have stood to fight. He had just stood alone against a multitude of Baal worshippers and won, but then fear overwhelmed him. He had become panic stricken. Is it not the same with some of us? Sometimes we stand strong in the Lord. But are there not moments when we too are overwhelmed by fear?

God Counsels Elijah

There in the wilderness and in a very depressed state of mind he cries to God saying, *'It is enough; now, O LORD, take my life, for I am no better than my fathers.'* Elijah was discouraged. He had come to a point in his life when things seemed to be working against him. There he was, being faithful to his calling and serving the Lord, yet his life was in danger. As far as he was concerned, he had remained obedient to the will of God. He had worked hard, but his future appeared to be nothing but bleak. He saw himself as the only faithful prophet left to fight against the evil of his time. Lonely and distressed, he had come to the conclusion that death would be a better alternative to life.

Is it not true that sometimes we too find ourselves in such a bind? We once counselled a teenager left with the burden of caring for his mother and family. Because his father was an irresponsible person, the young lad had to work hard to support the family. On several occasions, he told us that he would rather die than live. Life was becoming unbearable for him. That was the situation which Elijah was in. He was in a state of despair.

There is a peaceful beauty in the way God comforts Elijah. One would expect God to enter into an immediate dialogue with him, but this He does not do. Instead He sets the condition right for a meaningful ministry. He ministers first to the physical needs of Elijah.

God knew that Elijah would be of a better frame of mind for a divine encounter if his bodily needs were first attended to. He wanted Elijah to be at ease in the encounter. So He sends His angel who wakes Elijah and persuades him to eat. This He does twice reminding Elijah of his need to eat in order to be physically fit to meet with Him at Mount Horeb.

God is a wise physician. He comes to man in his moment of greatest helplessness and then restores, strengthens and prepares him for future usefulness. God renews our inner being so that we can serve Him better.

At Mount Horeb, God begins to counsel with Elijah. He says to Elijah, 'What are you doing here Elijah?' The question is asked not because God is unaware of Elijah's plight, but to allow Elijah an opportunity to articulate and release his frustrations. God wanted Elijah to experience an inner release that would free him from the bondage of fear, anger and disappointment.

So to the divine question, Elijah quickly responds by saying, *'I have been very zealous for the LORD, the God of hosts; for the sons of Israel have forsaken Thy covenant, torn down Thine altars and killed Thy prophets with the sword. And I alone am left; and they seek my life, to take it away.'* Elijah needed to release his suppressed feelings and God gave him the opportunity to do so.

Many of us have the same needs. I (Isaac) remember counselling a young lady who had been disappointed by her fiancée because she had found him flirting with another woman. She was in a state of anger and needed to unload and let her feelings go. As she began to share, she began to get more and more furious and, with the pitch of her voice rising with anger, she exclaimed, 'You men are all the same!' (an action for which she later apologized). She was embarrassed because it sounded as though she was scolding me. But after releasing her pent-up emotions, she felt good and was ready to work out her frustrations.

Elijah was distressed. He wanted God to know that he was really frustrated. He wanted God to know that he had come to the end of the road. He needed a release, and God allowed him the release.

Then God said to Elijah, *'Go forth, and stand on the mountain before the LORD.'* God wanted Elijah to know that He was an understanding God; that He was a God of compassion; that Elijah could tell Him how he felt. So He appeared to Elijah not in the great and strong wind, nor in the earthquake, nor in the fire, but in the sound of the gentle blowing, or as the Good News Bible puts it, *'the soft whisper of a voice'*.

God wanted Elijah to know that whatever the situation, He was still in charge. He could destroy the world by storm, earthquake or fire, but He was choosing not to. The sound of the gentle blowing was symbolic of God's compassion and love. It symbolized His willingness to delay punishment as long as mercy made it possible.

The manifestation of the strong wind, the earthquake and the fire were also symbolic representations of the state in which Elijah himself was in. Through these symbols, God was telling Elijah that these destructive feelings of anger and bitterness would be of no help to him. What he needed was to calm down and be quiet before the Lord.

Elijah Restored

Then for the second time, God says to Elijah, 'What are you doing here?' Again Elijah responds by saying the same thing. He repeats what he said the first time. But this time he is no longer in the same frame of mind as he was in the beginning. He is ready to be ministered to and to listen to what God has in store for him. It is in this point of receptivity that God not only instructs him and counsels him concerning his future, but He also assures Elijah that there are seven thousand others who have not bowed to Baal and that he is not the only faithful person left in the land. Having received counsel, Elijah goes on his way a renewed person.

God the Father comes to us in the same manner. In His gentleness He reaches out to us, comforts us, and meets us at our various points of need in ways most congenial to us. Such is the love of God for us. Ought not we to love and comfort one another?

God the Son

The caring heart of God is manifested in the person of Jesus. John the apostle understood the depth of this compassion when he quoted the words of Jesus, *'For God so loved the world, that He gave His only begotten Son, that whoever believes in Him should not perish, but have eternal life'* (John 3:16). In Jesus, God became flesh and dwelt among us (John 1:14). The eternal God has come to us in Jesus to be the Wonderful Counsellor. The prophecy pronounced by the prophet Isaiah that the child who would be born as the Messiah would also be the *'Wonderful Counsellor'* (Isaiah 9:6) became a reality with the birth of Christ.

As we read the pages of the Gospels, we cannot but agree with the proclamation that Jesus is truly the Wonderful Counsellor. Throughout His three-year ministry, Jesus counselled a multitude of people and brought comfort to their hearts. He counselled Nicodemus (John 3:1–21), the woman of Samaria (John 4:7–26), Mary and Martha (John 11:1–45), the rich young ruler (Matthew 19:16–22), His disciples (John 13–16) and countless others. Even when He knew that His end was coming and that the cross lay ahead of Him, He was not slow to comfort His disciples with these beautiful words,

> *'Let not your heart be troubled; believe in God, believe also in Me. In My Father's house are many dwelling places; if it were not so, I would have told you; for I go to prepare a place for you. And if I go and prepare a place for you, I will come again, and*

> *receive you to Myself; that where I am, there you may*
> *be also.'* (John 14:1–3)

Are these not beautiful words of our Wonderful Counsellor? Jesus has always been concerned about how we
feel. Redemption in Christ is also a release from the
bondage of negative feelings.

One of the most interesting encounters recorded for our
edification is Jesus' encounter with Zaccheus (Luke 19:1–
10).

Zaccheus the Troubled Tax Collector

We are told from Scripture that Zaccheus was a tax collector and he was very rich. Being a tax collector, he was not
a trusted person. His people regarded him a traitor
because he not only worked for the Romans who had
occupied Israel but was also overtaxing the people and
making them pay more than what was expected of them.
In these circumstances we can understand why the people
hated and despised him.

It must have been difficult for Zaccheus to survive in a
society that had ostracized him. He knew that he had to
be blamed for his own situation, yet he must have wished
that others would treat him with greater respect. In bringing suffering to his people, he himself was experiencing
the bitter pill of his own misdeeds.

Zaccheus was a bitter man. He hated being in the
company of fellow Jews because they treated him badly.
Together with these feelings of rejection and hurt were his
feelings of guilt. Deep within his heart he must have
known that he had wronged his people by betraying them
and abusing them. Zaccheus had all the wealth, but he
had no peace.

Zaccheus lived under heavy stress. He did not know
who his friends were or when his enemies would get a
him. He was an unpleasant person, and he had to b
unpleasant to survive. That was his occupational hazard

The people too kept their distance as they considered him unworthy of their fellowship. Zaccheus cared for no one, and so no one cared for him.

News reached him that Jesus was on His way to Jericho. He had heard that Jesus was a man of compassion and that Jesus was the friend of all – even tax collectors. He wanted to see Jesus and perhaps even meet with Him.

When Jesus entered Jericho, Zaccheus was determined to see Him. He knew that if he had to fight the crowd in order to get a glimpse of Jesus, he would never succeed. He was disadvantaged on two scores. Firstly, he was short, and it would be an impossible task peering over the shoulders of the crowd just to get a glimpse of Jesus. Secondly, the crowd knowing who he was would not hesitate to hurt him. In fact, they could take advantage of the situation and elbow him to injury.

Zaccheus had an idea. To avoid being hassled, he ran ahead of the crowd and climbed a sycamore tree to secure the best view for himself. Zaccheus must have been a desperate man to climb a tree. Any man of his position would not have done a thing like that. But Zaccheus needed to meet someone who could understand him; someone who would perhaps hear him out; someone who would accept him; someone who would be patient and who would make it possible for him to repent of his sins and receive the forgiveness of God. Jesus came and made repentance possible.

Jesus Ministers to Zaccheus

Approaching the tree where Zaccheus was, Jesus said, *'Zaccheus, hurry and come down for today I must stay at your house.'* A simple sentence of self-invitation, yet words of acceptance that Zaccheus had been waiting to hear.

Jesus could see that Zaccheus had a need. He knew that a man of Zaccheus' status would not climb a tree if he could help it. Jesus knew that Zaccheus needed inner healing; He knew that Zaccheus needed an inner cleansing and release that would set him free. Jesus met Zaccheus at his points of need.

Zaccheus Transformed

It was a special day for Zaccheus when he heard Jesus' request to visit with him. In fact the Bible says that Zaccheus rejoiced at the invitation. He was truly glad; he was really happy. For the first time, he felt accepted; for the first time, he felt cared for. Zaccheus felt humbled by the fact that a great Rabbi, a man of God, would visit with him and have fellowship with a sinner like him.

That encounter with Jesus, changed Zaccheus' life. We do not know what transpired during that encounter, but it must have been a life-changing encounter. He must have confessed and repented of his sins; he must have poured his heart out to Jesus and received His words of comfort; he must have spoken of his feelings of guilt and the hurt that he had suffered; he must have related to Jesus his feelings of loneliness and the pain of being ostracized. Jesus listened; Jesus loved; Jesus touched; Jesus healed; Jesus comforted. Zaccheus was changed.

Zaccheus said to Jesus, *'Behold, Lord, half of my possessions I will give to the poor, and if I have defrauded anyone of anything, I will give back four times as much.'* For someone with whom money meant a great deal, these words of Zaccheus were in fact words of repentance. Zaccheus was willing to repent and start life anew. He knew that restitution was necessary and he was willing to make the restitution. His values had also changed. Whilst once he allowed money to control him, now, he was willing to give it up in order for God to take first place in his life. Zaccheus had received ministry and inner healing. He had received the comfort of Jesus.

Jesus in hearing the words of Zaccheus said, *'Today salvation has come to this house because he, too, is a son of Abraham. For the Son of Man has come to seek and to save that which has been lost.'*

When a person receives wholeness through Christ, salvation has in fact come. The lost finds direction in Christ because He is the way; the lost finds self-realisation because Christ is the truth; the lost finds life in Christ because He is the Life. Is not Christ the Counsellor par excellence? Is He not the Comforter? As Jesus has set the example of care through the ministry of counselling, should we not also do likewise?

God the Holy Spirit

As we have seen the counselling heart of God and the counselling passion of Jesus, we recognise the same in the person of the Holy Spirit.

One of the most precious gifts that God has given to us is the gift of the Holy Spirit. In fact, the Christian's legacy is the Holy Spirit. Jesus in His departing speech to His disciples makes the following statements about the Holy Spirit:

> *'And I will ask the Father, and he will give you another Helper that He may be with you forever; that is the Spirit of truth whom the world cannot receive, because it does not behold Him or know Him, but you know Him because He abides with you and will be in you. I will not leave you as orphans; I will come to you.'* (John 14:16–18)

> *'But the Helper, the Holy Spirit, whom the Father will send in My name, He will teach you all things and bring to your remembrance all that I said to you.'* (John 14:26)

> *'When the Helper comes, whom I will send to you from the Father, that is the Spirit of truth, who proceeds from the Father, He will bear witness of Me, and you will bear witness also, because you have been with Me from the beginning.'* (John 15:26–27)

> '*But I tell you the truth, it is to your advantage that I go away; for if I do not go away, the Helper shall not come to you; but if I go, I will send Him to you. And He, when He comes, will convict the world concerning sin, and righteousness, and judgement; concerning sin, because they do not believe in Me; and concerning righteousness, because I go to the Father, and you no longer behold Me; and concerning judgement, because the ruler of this world has been judged.*'
>
> (John 16:7–11)

There are three significant things that Jesus mentions about the Holy Spirit.

Jesus' Replacement

The first is this – the Holy Spirit is Jesus' replacement. He is the other 'Helper', the other 'Comforter' or the other 'Counsellor'. That is to say, as Jesus is the Counsellor, the Holy Spirit is also a Counsellor (like Jesus). The Greek for the word 'Counsellor' is *parakletos* which can also be translated as 'Helper' or 'Comforter'. The word means – 'one called alongside to help'. The Holy Spirit ministers to us today as the Counsellor.

The Holy Spirit Indwells the Believer

The second of Jesus' teachings on the Holy Spirit is that the latter has a special relationship with the believer. He dwells within the believer. Indwelling the believer, He does three things.

1. The Teacher

Firstly, He functions as the Teacher. He helps us understand the truths of Christ; He helps us understand the Word of God; He helps us distinguish truth from falsehood; He puts in us a desire to learn the truth and continually hunger for His Word.

We have never stopped being amazed at how the understanding of God's Word can come to many in a moment of enlightenment. I (Shirley) had been trying to help a lady who had been steeped in drug addiction and immorality, to understand that God abhors sin. She had come seeking help from the church as a non-Christian who wanted whatever help we could offer. She was also interested in the Gospel and clearly wanted to be a follower of Christ. However, it was difficult to help her understand God's love as well as God's abhorrence of sin. She argued that if God loves her, and she has on occasions experienced the reality of God's love in her life, then God would forgive her even if she continued to sin. She needed to be convicted of the evil of sin and the certainty of the penalty of sin (Romans 6:23). It was a sudden revelation for her when one day she called me on the phone and said, 'Mrs Lim, I've just understood something that God says in His Word. Psalm 66:18 says if I regard wickedness in my heart, the Lord will not hear me. That's what you've been trying to say, right?' As a result of the work of the Holy Spirit in teaching this lady the truth of Scripture, she began a quest for a closer knowledge of the Word. She bought Christian literature, joined Bible courses and the last time I saw her, she was asking for back issues of *Our Daily Bread* which had become her favourite devotional guide.

2. *The Reminder*

Secondly, the Holy Spirit functions as One who reminds. He brings to our remembrance what Christ has taught us; He brings to our remembrance what pleases Christ; He brings to our remembrance the will of Christ; He brings to our remembrance the teachings of Christ; He brings to our remembrance the love of Christ for us.

A friend who used to be active in Christian work in his youth shared with us his experience of drifting away from the Lord and living a life of self-reliance in building up a career. However, he said that all the time, it seemed as if God had never left him. He had finally made his way back to Church, a humbled man. 'I'm glad I've come back to the Lord,' he said, 'I'm sure the Lord has never left me because each time I saw a church or a Christian book shop, I was reminded of the time when I felt secure in the love of God. I thought then that it was just a teenage fantasy on my part but now I know that what I had was real and I'll never let it go again!'

3. The Disturber of our Conscience

Thirdly, the Holy Spirit functions as the Disturber of our Conscience. He convicts us of sin. When we feel restless and when our conscience seems to disturb us, it is because the Holy Spirit is working within us. He convicts us also of righteousness, reminding us that it is the righteousness of Christ and His blood that will blot out all our transgressions and help us stand as righteous before God. He convicts us of judgement, reminding us that evil will be condemned and those who stand on the side of evil will be judged.

The Holy Spirit bears Witness of Christ

Finally, Jesus teaches us that the Holy Spirit bears witness of Christ. That is to say, in all events and trials of life, the Holy Spirit points us to Jesus as the answer to all our needs. He reminds us that Jesus came to earth to die on the cross for us so that we can experience healing and wholeness in Him. The Holy Spirit leads us to the Wonderful Counsellor that we may receive comfort, strength and help in our time of need. He brings us to Jesus that we may receive His healing balm in our time of pain.

The Holy Spirit Counsels

How does the Holy Spirit counsel? The Holy Spirit counsels in the quietness of our hearts, bringing grace and peace in fullest measure (1 Peter 1:2). The Holy Spirit in His work of sanctification moulds us and makes us the person God wants us to be. The Holy Spirit as Counsellor sensitizes our conscience so that we are able to discern right from wrong. Through His quiet promptings we are guided in the path of righteousness.

The Holy Spirit comes to us in our moments of distress and trials and intercedes for us. In Romans 8:26–27, Paul says, *'And in the same way the Spirit also helps our weakness; for we do not know how to pray as we should, but the Spirit Himself intercedes for us with groanings too deep for words; and He who searches the hearts knows what the mind of the Spirit is, because He intercedes for the saints according to the will of God.'* The Holy Spirit counsels with us in troubled moments.

The Spirit of Truth

The Holy Spirit is not only the Counsellor, but also the Spirit of Truth. Wholeness of mind and spirit is possible when we face the truth concerning ourselves and our condition. When the Holy Spirit works in our lives, He points to us areas in our lives that are not right in God's sight. He then leads us to repentance and to a right relationship with God.

The example of the Triune God is before us. We as his people are called to spread the Gospel of hope to all. As the Triune Counsellor brings comfort and peace to all in distress, He invites us to do likewise.

Chapter 3

A Body Ministry

'I am desperate, it's like death is the only way out. They say that your church may be able to help me, so I decided to come.' Molly was almost hysterical with anguish. She was caught in a marriage that didn't work. Her own past contributed to the marriage relationship as she had been ill-treated by uncaring, mercenary parents who had married her off for money. Her husband was unable to handle a difficult, attention-seeking wife and became an alcoholic who battered her and sexually abused her in fits of anger. Molly had run away from home and left her husband and children. 'I miss them,' she cried her heart out, 'not my husband – it's my children. When I look at the parents down the road bringing their children to McDonald's, I just feel like ending my life – I feel so guilty ... and yet I'll never go back, not to be treated like an animal!'

Molly received counsel and did return home. The personal ministry of the Lord was so real that she went home within days, a changed person. We received a call from her husband a couple of weeks later. He wanted to thank us and find out what Molly meant by having been healed by God. 'She's so different now, she's even patient and caring. I'd like to attend church with her but I'll have to bring my children along – may I?' Of course he could! How we marvelled at God's work in answering our prayers! He came to see us in slippers, a humble man.

Today, after a series of fierce spiritual battles and heart-rending emotional conflicts, the couple has received healing of the wounds of those personal battles. They have found acceptance and ministry in a church and are both serving the Lord with joy in their hearts in different capacities in that church. Molly left her secular job and became a full-time clerk in a Christian organisation.

The Bible speaks of the Church as a community of care and ministry. There are many Mollys who need ministry of the same nature. Are we there to help? What does the Bible say about Body ministry? Let's begin with Jesus.

The Prayer of Jesus

It has always been the desire of Jesus that His followers exude a fragrance and beauty that would reflect the oneness of the Church. In His high priestly prayer in John 17:20–23, He prays:

> *'I do not ask on behalf of these alone, but for those also who believe in Me through their word; that they may all be one; even as Thou, Father, art in Me, and I in Thee, that they also may be in Us; that the world may believe that Thou didst send Me. And the glory which Thou hast given Me I have given to them; that they may be one, just as We are one; I in them, and Thou in Me, that they may be perfected in unity; that the world may know that Thou didst send Me, and didst love them, even as Thou didst love Me.'*

It is apparent from this prayer that Christian witness is strongest when the Church works in unity as a demonstration of the love of God within its fellowship. But the Church can only reflect that oneness if God's people are of one mind, one heart and one spirit. There is a need for God's people to be right both with Him and with their fellow men. There is a need for a ministry of reconciliation that will reconcile man to God, man to each other, and man to himself.

Jesus knew that wholeness of mind and spirit was an important prerequisite for the wholeness of His church. He knew that if His disciples were to serve Him well and bring the Gospel to the ends of the earth, they needed to be whole persons. The effectiveness of their ministry depended on their degree of wholeness. He wanted to see each of his disciples empowered for service (Acts 1:8).

Jesus Counsels Peter

Jesus' concern for the wholeness of His disciples is well illustrated in His encounter with Peter after the resurrection (John 21).

You will remember that Peter had denied Jesus three times. The days that followed must have been difficult days for Peter as the memory of those awful episodes haunted him. Although he had wept bitterly for denying the Lord (Luke 22:62), he had not forgiven himself for his failings, nor was he certain that the Lord had forgiven him. There was within him a sense of guilt that needed to be dealt with; he needed an assurance of acceptance by the Lord Himself if he were to be effective in His service again.

When the resurrected Christ met Peter on the shores of the Sea of Tiberias, He knew that the only way Peter could be restored to wholeness of mind and spirit was to deal with his feelings of guilt. Peter had to be released from his sense of guilt and unworthiness if he were to be used in effective service. Peter's confidence in himself had to be restored; he had to be assured that Jesus could still rely on him.

It was an uneasy moment when Jesus posed the question, *'Simon, son of John, do you love me more than these?'* It is interesting to note the drift of the conversation in which Jesus seemed to be asking Peter the same question three times. Let us take a look at the dialogue:

First time

Jesus: *'Simon, son of John, do you love* (agapao) *me more than these?'*

Peter: *'Yes Lord; You know that I love* (phileo) *You.'*

Jesus: *'Tend my lambs.'*

Second time

Jesus: *'Simon, son of John, do you love* (agapao) *Me?'*

Peter: *'Yes, Lord; You know that I love* (phileo) *You.'*

Jesus: *'Shepherd My Sheep.'*

Third time

Jesus: *'Simon, son of John, do you love* (phileo) *me?'*

Peter: *'Lord, You know all things; You know that I love* (phileo) *You.'*

Jesus: *'Tend My Sheep.'*

Jesus in asking Peter three times *'... do you love me ...'* was allowing Peter the opportunity to affirm his love for Him. But Peter could not in all honesty say that he loved the Lord in the *agape* manner.

You will note in the above dialogue that two Greek words *agapao* and *phileo* are used in place of our one English word love. Both *agapao* and *phileo* are translated as 'love' in the above passage. *Agapao* is a love that is unconditional. It is a pure unselfish love that is without ulterior motives. *Phileo* however is a love that is not of the same intensity as *agapao*. It is a love that is mutual. It is a brotherly or sisterly sort of love. It is a love that is conditional.

Peter could only love the Lord with *phileo* love. Yet, Jesus was willing to accept Peter's love at that level when he eventually asked the question, *'Simon, son of John, do you love* (phileo) *me?'* By the very question Jesus was in fact saying to Simon, 'I love you even when you are unable to love me with the same intensity as my love for you. And because I love (*agapao*) you and trust you, I am going to give you an important responsibility. Shepherd my sheep.'

The exercise did three things for Peter. Firstly, it allowed Peter to regain the feeling of acceptance. Peter's fear was that Jesus would reject him for his failures but Jesus accepted him in spite of the fact that he had denied his Master three times. Secondly, it allowed Peter the opportunity to be honest with himself and with the Lord. Instead of being impulsive and wanting always to impress Jesus, Peter could now express his true self. He could say that he loved Jesus but not in the *agape* manner. Thirdly, Jesus restored Peter's sense of worth when He told him to '*feed the lambs*'. Jesus had considered him still useful in His service.

Peter had been ministered to; inner healing had taken place and henceforth he was ready to minister to others as well. Peter had experienced the compassion and comfort of Jesus and he was not to forget that. This could be seen in the way he organised the early church.

After the outpouring of the Holy Spirit at Pentecost and the conversion of three thousand persons through the preaching of Peter's sermon, caring groups were formed. These groups reflected a love that was at the very heart of Jesus. The Bible says that '*all those who had believed were together and had all things in common; and they began selling their property and possessions, and were sharing with all, as anyone had need ... And the Lord was adding to their number day by day those who were being saved*' (Acts 2:44, 45, 47). The prayer of Jesus had become a reality. The oneness of fellowship was evident as the early Christians took pains to care for one another. Each was accepted just as he or she was and helped to become what Christ wanted him or her to be.

People were being drawn to the new 'way' because they could see the transformation that was taking place in the lives of those who had become Christians. The Church was growing because those who were responding not only experienced a renewal of life; they also experienced a new dimension of love. They found themselves being helped, comforted and ministered to by the early disciples. Their caring concern was also reflected in Acts 6 when the widows of the Hellenistic Jews complained against the native Hebrews for being partial in the distribution of daily rations. The apostles took immediate action and summoned the church to appoint seven deacons to handle the problem. Some ministering and counselling must have taken place to bring about reconciliation and peace. There was here the building up of community wholeness.

It must have been Peter's joy to see the church functioning as a community of care. Several years later while writing to the Christians in Asia Minor he expressed the same concern by describing the Church as a spiritual house made up of living stones with Christ as the choice cornerstone (1 Peter 2:4–8).

Living Stones

In 1 Peter 2:4–5, Peter talks about Christians as living stones being built up into a spiritual house. The image of Christians as living stones is a very interesting image. In fact it takes its lead from Christ who is the Living Stone rejected by man, yet choice and precious in the sight of God.

When Peter talked about the Church as composed of living stones, he must have recognized the importance of every stone in the very building of the spiritual house. As Jesus, the Living Stone was choice and precious in God's sight, he saw every Christian as also choice and precious in God's sight.

We as individual Christians are called to avail ourselves to the Lord as *'living stones'* so that we may collectively be *'built up as a spiritual house for a holy priesthood, to offer up spiritual sacrifices acceptable to God through Jesus*

Christ' (1 Peter 2:5). We are to be like stones in a building, put together in such a way as to lend support to others, while we ourselves rest on others. Only in this way can we build a spiritual house that offers up spiritual sacrifices acceptable to God. In other words, as **living stones**, we are told to touch each other's lives in supportive ministry. The example is laid down for us in Christ who has shared His Life with us as the **Stone**.

Bernard Thomson in his book *Good Samaritan Faith* shared his personal dream of what a local church could be.[1] He writes,

> 'I dreamed of a local church that would help every member feel he or she belonged to a caring community. A church in which all areas of one's life were valued. A church which surrounded all members with the love of Christ.
>
> 'I dreamed of a local church which freed each person to use all of his or her God-given gifts. A church which encouraged everyone to reach his or her full spiritual maturity in Christ. This caring local church would also care about the surrounding community.
>
> 'The church members would have God's mission in their hearts. They would get to know their neighbours, and share their love for God through attractive, Christ-centred, genuinely caring life-styles.'

These dreams can come about when living stones begin to rest on each other and are themselves rested on. As we begin to work out an ever-widening network of care and counselling amongst lay persons, we see more and more of the power of God at work in individual lives. Many more are ministered to by the grace and power of the Holy Spirit and many more receive the joy of service. This symbiotic relationship, this mutual ministry that blesses the giver as well as the receiver, is God's design for the Church.

The Body of Christ

Like Peter, the Apostle Paul saw the importance of the Church as a supportive community when he spoke of the Church as the Body of Christ. He saw the Church as not composed of one part of the body but of many parts. He saw each part as integral to the function of the whole. He saw every member of the Body doing its part under the direction of the Head so that the whole Body could function beautifully as a complete unit.

Paul talked about the gifts of the Holy Spirit bestowed on believers as means by which the whole Body could function in supportive ministry. The variety of gifts endowed upon the various participants of the Body meant that ministries needed to complement each other. Those with problems could find within the Body a company of people who could assist them in their search for healing and wholeness. Talking about the gifts of the Spirit, Paul writes in 1 Corinthians 12:7–11

> *'But to each one is given the manifestation of the Spirit for the common good. For to one is given the word of wisdom through the Spirit, and to another the word of knowledge according to the same Spirit; to another faith by the same Spirit, and to another gifts of healing by the one Spirit, and to another the effecting of miracles, and to another prophecy, and to another the distinguishing of spirits, to another various kinds of tongues, and to another the interpretation of tongues. But one and the same Spirit works all these things distributing to each one individually just as He wills.'*

To further highlight the variety of gifts within the Body, Paul writing to the Church in Ephesus said, *'He gave some as apostles, some as evangelists, and some as pastors and teachers, for the equipping of the saints for the work of service, to the building up of the Body of Christ'* (Ephesians 4:11–12).

It is evident that God has given us the Church so that we can minister to each other. The Church needs to be built up for ministry and Paul gives a clear directive for spiritual leaders to build up the Body by working together in unity to equip the saints for the work of ministry.

In the context of Christian counselling and care, it is imperative or necessary for spiritual leaders to consider seriously their roles as leaders and trainers of counsellors in response to Christ's call to the Church to be the centre of ministry. Also, members of the body who do not see themselves as leaders are nonetheless to respond to the high calling of being ministers of the Lord, and to avail themselves to be equipped for the ministry.

The imperative in Scripture for all born-again Christians to provide mutual support and comfort is clear. In 2 Corinthians 1:4, Paul argues that as we have received comfort from God, we can by the power of that comfort also be a comfort to others. The verse reads, *'(God) who comforts us in all our affliction so that we may be able to comfort those who are in any affliction with the comfort with which we ourselves are comforted by God.'* The stress here is in the comfort of God that all can experience. We as Christians are called to share the comfort of God.

God's Directive to the Church

Scripture outlines clearly the call to the whole church to be involved in the *'ministry of reconciliation'* (2 Corinthians 5:18). The individual Christian is exhorted not to look only to his own needs but also to the needs of others (Philippians 2:4). There are direct injunctions in Scripture for every Christian to *'bear one another's burdens, and thus fulfil the law of Christ'* (Galatians 6:2). We are also told to be always ready to comfort the troubled with the comfort that we ourselves have received from

God. Pastors and spiritual leaders are specifically told to equip God's people for works of service (Ephesians 4:11–12).

Howard Clinebell outlines the role of the pastors in the ministry of counselling in these words, 'Our job is to train, inspire, guide, coach, and work alongside the lay ministers as "teachers of teachers", "pastors of pastors" and "counsellors of counsellors"'.[2]

God's plan for the Church is for it to be a vibrant community that provides ministry within, in a symbiotic 'give and take' spirit of mutual ministries, as well as a community that provides ministry in reaching out to those who are not yet within the Christian community. The more this is done, the more relevant it will be as Christ's ambassador in meeting the needs of people.

A Further Imperative

A further imperative for the ministry of counselling can be found in Paul's letter to the Church in Thessalonica. He says in 1 Thessalonians 5:14, '*And we* **urge** *(parakaleo)* *you, brethren,* **admonish** *(noutheteo) the unruly,* **encourage** *(parmutheomai) the faint-hearted,* **help** *(antechomai) the weak, be* **patient** *(makrothumeo) with all men.*'

It is interesting to note that there are five variations of Greek verbs on counselling found in this verse. They are *parakaleo* (to urge), *noutheteo* (to admonish), *paramutheomai* (to encourage), *antechomai* (to help), and *makrothumeo* (to be patient). The verb *parakaleo* which is also used in Romans 12:1; 15:30, and in 2 Corinthians 1:4 means 'to beseech', 'to exhort', or 'to encourage', or 'to comfort'. It means to bring a word of exhortation, encouragement or comfort to one in need. This is precisely what we do in counselling.

The second verb *noutheteo* means 'to warn', 'to admonish', or 'to confront'. The verb which is also found in 1 Corinthians 4:14 and Colossians 3:16 has inherent in its meaning the idea of admonishing with the intention of bringing about change in a person's lifestyle. This is sometimes done in counselling when the unruly, the stubborn and the undisciplined need to be admonished in order that wholeness and healing can take place.

The third verb is *paramutheomai*. It means to cheer or to encourage or to console those who are depressed or discouraged (1 Thessalonians 2:11,12). The fourth verb *antechomai* means 'to cling', 'to hold fast' or 'to take an interest in'. It has to do with giving spiritual and emotional support to one in need. The fifth verb is the word *makrothumeo* which means 'to be patient' (Matthew 18:26, 29; James 5:7; Hebrews 6:15). It can be applied to the need for patience in the ministry of counselling.

This verse in itself supports the need for a ministry of counselling. It is useful for us to note that these five verbs represent five aspects of counselling as they are modes that we intermittently adopt in the practice of counselling.

The Distinguishing Marks of a Christian Church

Love and Unity

We as Christians are also called to proclaim God's love. One of the distinguishing marks of a Christian Church is love (John 13:35). It is love not only for a fellow Christian, but love for others as well. You will remember that the imperative for the Christian to be Christ's ambassador of love is well illustrated in the parable of the Good Samaritan (Luke 10:30–37). This need to bring comfort to others and to express the caring compassion of the Lord to the needy is also affirmed in Matthew 25. Matthew 25 categorically states that what separates the sheep from the goats is the compassion that is expressed for those who are least amongst us. It is certainly a caustic reminder for all Christians that the acid test of our faith in the Lord is that flow of compassion for the least amongst us.

If we say that we love God, then our love for those in need must also be evident. To allow our hearts to be hardened, and our compassion for the suffering blocked, is to stray from the imperatives of our Lord. The natural end therefore as alluded to in Matthew 25 is eternal punishment. However, for those who would allow God's love to motivate and empower them to reach out to the least amongst us, they would in fact be ministering to the Christ who says, *'to the extent that you did it to one of these brothers of Mine, even the least of them, you did it to Me'* (Matthew 25:40).

We can see from the above that the Bible is far from ambivalent over the question of a ministry of care and comfort. It is a ministry that all Christians in the Body of Christ are commissioned to be involved in. Whilst we can see that many Christians have indeed been practising a ministry of love and support in their own quiet way as friends, counsellors, mentors, and the like, there is also a need for the local church to work out in an increasingly succinct and focused way an operational network for the better exercise of spiritual gifts within the context of the Church.

While it is important for individual Christians to minister to others in their own personal capacities, we see the need for Christians to serve in conjunction with the Church as the basis of a caring community. This urgency is felt as we see the limitations of individual efforts alone in the ministry of care and counselling and the imperative that is set forth in Scripture for a concerted effort in such a ministry by the Body of Christ.

Sharing and Caring

The Church, if it is to be a centre of care, must minister to the personal needs of those who come, whatever their needs may be. There must be an experience of sharing and caring. This is the key to Church growth in the full sense of the word – where the church will increase in numbers as well as in the enrichment of the lives of individual members. However, it is sad to note that often, as Gary Collins so aptly puts it, '... the body of believers, which has potential for being a dynamic growth-producing fellowship, too often degenerates into a listless, rigid group of people who never admit to having needs or problems, attend services out of habit, leave most of the action to an overburdened pastor. Such a picture is overstated, perhaps, but for many people the local church really isn't very helpful or meaningful. This surely was not Christ's intention when the Church was first established.'[3]

In a Methodist church we were invited to in the United States, a poised, statuesque lady discussed with us, the concept of sharing and caring in the church. The lady explained how she found this concept of mutual personal ministry within the Church, quite fascinating. As she intellectualised over the issue in educated and polished fluency, she suddenly broke down in tears and confessed a feeling that she had been trying to hide for months. Since the death of her husband about half a year before she had been lonely and broken and unable to handle the void she felt in her life. However, no one in her church was aware of how she felt because of her outward composure, which she was careful to maintain on Sundays after the services. How glad she was to be able to lay down that heavy burden of being always strong, poised and victorious.

This fallacy that the Christian is one who cannot be shaken by circumstances and adverse events, is Satan's way of preventing the effectual ministries of members of Christ's Body. Gritting one's teeth and maintaining a good front is not the way to maintain an effective witness. It is true that God does in fact grant us the grace for every trial and does give us a peace that passeth understanding in times of trouble. However, it is also true that He often breaks us to mould us into His likeness. Mutual loving support during times of need is God's way of building up His People in His bond of love.

Mission and Outreach

The mission of the Church is to declare the Good News of the Gospel to all men. This can also be communicated through the means of social outreach. It means ministering to all who would approach the Church for help and assistance.

Isaac raised his eyebrows in initial surprise, 'Was that the lady you spoke to last week?' He could hardly recognise Susie as she walked out of the counselling room after a session with me (Shirley). She had been referred to us a few months before, as a dishevelled looking, shifty-eyed lady who had been broken and hardened by years of dishonest immoral living, and had been released from prison two days earlier. She had heard of Jesus through the prison services and wanted to make a clean start upon release. The two months had been a hard tussle with sin. She tried to follow the ways of the Lord and shun sin but failed. She came back for help again, and sinned again. Finally, the breakthrough came. The Lord helped her to see that immoral living was no game and gave her a resolve to keep away. Healing had begun. From the depression and deception she was deeply trapped in, she began to smile a smile of freedom. The thick stench that used to pervade the air around her had left. She looked neat and radiant, almost beautiful. Two years later, she was still regularly attending church and successfully completed Bible study and nurture courses. On the day of her baptism, we could see that the healing process that had begun was still continuing. She had received help not only from me, but also from the Church as a community of care.

'My story is even more astounding, isn't it?' Jane remarked. 'I was actually under psychiatric help for months for my depression. I thought I was going mad – I was getting so negative. I didn't know the Lord then. My eyes would roll up on their own and I would get these flashes of anger – I could have killed my husband and children. Look at me today – Rev. Lim says he can hardly recognise me!'

These are all real experiences. These persons have not only been ministered to by us but also by others in the church. They have found meaning not only because Christ has accepted them and we have accepted them, but their respective churches have been supportive as well. We praise God for that.

The identities of the persons involved as shared above and in the following pages have been blurred by the changing of names and specific details. However, they are persons who will be quite happy to share person-to-person with you. It is essential, in a book like this, to preserve the identities, so as not to distract attention from the fact that it is the work of God, through the obedience of His people, that wholeness of mind and spirit can be restored to the suffering. God can do likewise and more for any one. Persons within the Body of Christ must be allowed to lose their old identities and stigmas and begin life anew in the Lord. The church that is a centre of gossip and censure is not God's healing community. But a church that accepts the repentant no matter what their background, is a place of Comfort and Refuge where Christ's Love and stand-ards are taught and encouraged.

God is looking to you to give a helping hand. The Church needs Christians who can share in bringing the joy of the Lord to those who are struggling through life and help them into a new life of purity and truth in Christ. The needy are looking for a concerned someone who will be that Good Samaritan to help them in their battered state. Will you be that someone?

The Christian has the privilege of looking at himself as the helper whom God can use. He should seek not so much to be helped but to help. Yet in helping he is helped. Was not Saint Francis of Assisi right when he prayed:

'Lord make me an instrument of thy peace
Where there is hatred, let me sow love,
Where there is injury, pardon,
Where there is doubt, faith,
Where there is despair, hope,
Where there is darkness, light,
Where there is sadness, joy.
O Divine Master,
Grant that I may not so much seek
To be consoled, as to console,
To be understood, as to understand,
To be loved, as to love;
For it is in giving that we receive,
It is in pardoning that we are pardoned,
And it is in dying that we are born to Eternal Life.'

Would it not be wonderful if every member of God's Church becomes an instrument of His Peace and Comfort?

Chapter 4

A Holistic Ministry

Mei, a lady in her late thirties had come to see me (Isaac). She had been suffering from chest pains and breathlessness although the doctors could not find anything really wrong with her. Lately, the fear of death had also come upon her and she would be drenched with cold sweat in these moments of panic. Mei had told me that she had consulted not only her doctor, but also a psychiatrist but to no avail.

I took time to minister to her over a few sessions. I knew there were things in her life that remained unresolved. With every session I got to know more about her and it was not till the third session that she was willing to confess what was truly disturbing her.

Mei grew up as a very religious girl. When she was in her early twenties, she befriended a married man. The relationship was at first platonic but soon feelings developed and she eventually found herself having an affair with him. Although she eventually broke off with this man, her guilt feelings remained. Being religious, she had feared the wrath of God upon her and although she had confessed to God her sins, she was still afraid that God would punish her for her misdeeds. Her fear and guilt over a period of several years had resulted in her ailments.

There are many like Mei who suffer from sickness and

disease as a result of unresolved feelings of guilt. It is important to remind ourselves that what goes on in the realm of our minds and emotions does in fact affect our bodies. Mei had guilt feelings that remained resident in her subconscious and which surfaced intermittently creating havoc both in her mind and body.

The Trinity of Man

In a person-centred ministry, there is a need to understand the nature of man. As such, we will move now into a discussion of the composition or make-up of man in the light of Scripture. This we hope will help us in the richer understanding of the need for a ministry of healing and wholeness.

We need to realize that wholeness involves the working of the soul, spirit and body in proper harmony. There must be a proper working together of the soul and body, the body and the spirit, the spirit and the soul in their varied combinations.

Christian counselling is holistic. A holistic ministry addresses all the three component parts of a person – the **body, soul** and **spirit**. We need to recognise that God made man with these three basic component parts. In Genesis 2:7, we read, *'Then the Lord God formed man of the dust from the ground (**body**), and breathed into his nostrils the breath of life (**spirit**); and man became a living being (**soul**).'*[1] Paul in the New Testament affirms the trinity of man in his discussion on sanctification. He says in 1 Thessalonians 5:23, *'Now may the God of peace Himself sanctify you entirely; and may your **spirit** and **soul** and **body** be preserved complete, without blame at the coming of our Lord Jesus Christ.'*

It is important for us to remember that the goal of Christian counselling is to enable the counsellee to receive wholeness of body, soul and spirit. The Bible tells us that we are made in the image or likeness of God (Genesis

1:27), but through sin, that image has become tarnished. However, God through Christ has made it possible for us to have His image restored in us. The Apostle Paul says, *'Therefore if any man is in Christ, he is a new creature; the old things passed away; behold new things have come'* (2 Corinthians 5:17). We are made new in Christ Jesus. Consequently, the best gift a Christian counsellor can offer his counsellee is Jesus Christ.

It is apparent from the above texts that the body, spirit and soul are significant component parts of the human person. Although these parts appear as separate entities they are in fact intricately linked to form the living being. These three component parts are so interrelated and inter-dependent that wholeness and health are dependent on the well-being of all the component parts.

When one part of this tripartite composition of man is affected, the rest are invariably involved. For instance, when a person is physically sick, his personality which is his soul gets affected. He will not be as vibrant and posi-tive as he normally would be. If his soul is disturbed, his body will be affected, as in the case of one who is going through a period of depression. If a person is spiritually sick, his soul and body are also affected. As such, care in counselling is the care of the body, the soul and the spirit.

Body

The New Testament word for body is *soma*. It is interest-ing to note that there is no Hebrew equivalent for *soma*. A Hebrew word that is commonly used to denote body is the word *basar*. Yet, *basar* is not so much 'soma' but *sarx* a Greek word for flesh. It describes man in his weakness and mortality.[2]

The New Testament talks about man as a body-soul-spirit unit. He lives and moves and has his being in his body. His ultimate goal as a Christian is eternal life which is the eternal existence of the soul-spirit and the resurrected body (1 Corinthians 15:50–58) in the presence of Christ. Yet he knows that the *soma* made of earthly substance would decay, and his dependence for a resurrected body is in God. The Apostle Paul in 2 Corinthians 5:1 says, *'For we know that if the earthly tent which is our house is torn down, we have a building from God, a house not made with hands, eternal in the heavens.'*

The Body Houses the Spirit-Soul

Paul, in 2 Corinthians 5:1, likens the body to a tent. The implication of this passage is that the shell in which our soul and spirit dwell is the body. This is the part of the trinity of man that will decay and perish with time. Death brings about a complete cessation of the body with all its functions and the spirit-soul returns to be with God only to be given a spiritual body fit for heavenly life on the day of resurrection.

The Body Affects the Soul

As the body is the visible expression of the human person, the state of his inner being is reflected by the outward presentation of himself. What we see on the outside of a person is often a reflection of what is happening inside.

Sometimes however, the external body, affects the inner man. What is seen on the outside in terms of a physical presentation, may affect a person's self-concept. That is to say, a person's physical deformities and imperfections sometimes affect his personality and emotional well-being. A person who is physically handicapped or is physically unattractive for example, may feel inadequate. There is a tendency for the less well endowed to be sensitive about their appearance and suffer emotional setbacks.

The Body Must be Cared for

The body also affects the soul and the spirit when it is neglected and uncared for. When we fail to feed the body or nourish it adequately, we destroy our body and this affects our soul and spirit as well.

In the context of ministry to persons holistically, we need to consider ways of ministering to those suffering from hunger, illness, stress-related ailments, and ailments related to obsessions such as smoking, drinking, etc. There is a need for the local church to address these issues of genuine physical needs and to consider means such as education, subsistence aid, medical aid or assistance, and personal care and supervision for counsellees whose needs are principally physical.

One can see therefore, the counselling ministry to be a ministry of care augmented by an effective welfare system which aims at meeting basic physical needs. The scriptural injunction in Matthew 25, to care for the hungry, the thirsty, the imprisoned, the destitute, etc. is an imperative, not only for the individual Christian, but also for the Church as the collective body. It is only in so far as our love for the Lord is demonstrated in our care for suffering people that this professed love is seen as genuine. In other words, God's love and compassion for us if genuinely felt will certainly be expressed as a deep concern for the needs of others, particularly, the least amongst us.

Immoral Acts Affect the Soul

Another way in which the body affects the soul and spirit is through immoral acts. As the Apostle Paul puts it, the body is not for immorality but for the Lord (1 Corinthians 6:13). There is a kind of built-in divine mechanism within us that causes us to react negatively to immorality. Whether we are Christian or not, immorality is an unacceptable code of behaviour and our inner persons get disturbed when we indulge in these activities.

A young lady once came to see me (Shirley) with a problem of guilt. For years she had been indulging in fornication and the person whom she thought would marry her decided to break the relationship. Because of the break-up, she began to despise herself as cheap and stupid; she could not forgive herself and feared that she would not be able to find a mate who would accept her and her past. Her inability to handle her situation resulted in a mental disorder. She began to spend more time in the bathroom soaping herself thoroughly and claiming that her body was not clean enough.

Apparently, she could not handle her guilt feelings. By washing herself over and over again she was symbolically attempting to rid herself of her unclean past. Was not the Apostle Paul right when he said,

> *'Flee immorality. Every other sin that a man commits is outside the body, but the immoral man sins against his own body. Or do you not know that your body is a temple of the Holy Spirit who is in you, whom you have from God, and that you are not your own? For you have been bought with a price: therefore glorify God in your body.'* (1 Corinthians 6:18–20)

Paul raises three important points in this passage. The first is this. The immoral man sins against his own body. That is to say, whenever we commit immoral acts, we are condemning our own bodies. We are going against the very grain of moral living and the natural laws of God. The defiling of the body invariably affects the condition of the soul and spirit. When we indulge in immorality, we sin against both our soul and spirit.

Secondly, the body is a temple of the Holy Spirit. When a Christian is 'born again' he becomes a temple of the Holy Spirit. For the Christian, to defile the body is to desecrate the residence of the Holy Spirit. He grieves the Holy Spirit and creates a chasm in his relationship with the Holy Spirit. A constant sinning against the body will affect his usefulness as a Christian witness because the Holy Spirit who is deeply grieved cannot function in a body that seeks to resist His influence. King David, after he had been rebuked by Nathan the prophet for committing adultery with Bathsheba, prayed that the Holy Spirit would not depart from him. In repentance he cried,

> *'Create in me a clean heart, O God,*
> *And renew a steadfast spirit within me.*
> *Do not cast me away from Thy presence,*
> *And do not take Thy Holy Spirit from me.'*
>
> (Psalm 51:10–11)

A Christian who persists in sinning against his body through immoral acts will soon find himself spiritually wanting.

Thirdly, we have been bought with a price. Jesus died on the cross, not only in order that our souls might be delivered from the bondage of sin, but that our physical bodies might also experience wholeness and healing (Isaiah 53:4, 5). It is by His 'stripes' that we are healed. Because we have been bought with a price through the blood of Christ at Calvary, we are precious unto the Lord. In other words, a healthy body together with a soul influenced by the Holy Spirit through the spirit of man provides for health and wholeness.

Soul

One of the most difficult differentiations to make is between the soul and spirit of man. Although there is a distinction between the soul and the spirit, the terms are often used interchangeably (e.g. Luke 1:46–47) so that what is said of the soul holds true also of the spirit. However, there are times when Scripture differentiates between the soul and spirit, as in Hebrews 4:12, where God's word is able to divide man's soul and spirit. Richard Taylor refers to the spirit as that aspect of the soul which can be said to be Godward in nature, and the soul as that aspect of the spirit which is outward and manward.[3] He bases his distinction on Paul's discussion of the *'natural man'* and the *'spiritual man'* in 1 Corinthians 2:13–15. He says,

> 'The natural person – obviously the unregenerated – is the *psychikos* or 'soulish' person. He is alive in soul but not in spirit. His horizontal life is intact, but the vertical dimension of his nature is dead (or dormant). The person's spirit must be quickened by the Holy Spirit in regeneration.[4]

The Hebrew word for soul is *nepes*. It means 'breathe' and as such denotes life. The soul is understood in terms of a living person. A living soul is a living person. It is the individual – man himself. The Greek word for soul is *psyche*. Like *nepes*, it refers to the whole person (Acts 2:43; 3:23).

What is the Soul?

The soul (*psyche*) is that part of man which relates to his thoughts, feelings (Job 30:25; Psalm 86:4; Jeremiah 13:17; Ephesians 6:6) and will (Genesis 49:6; Job 7:15; Psalm 119:129, 167) in day-to-day living. Hence the intellectual, emotional and volitional aspects of man's life affect the well-being of the soul. The soul is sometimes referred to as the immaterial part of man (Matthew 10:28).

The soul is the psychological aspect of man that has to be ministered to as this is where the struggle between self and God principally lies. Paul refers in Romans 7:19 to that part of his human nature that hampers the performing of God's will. He laments, *'For the good that I wish, I do not do; but I practise the very evil that I do not wish.'* Ministering to the soul of man, involves a deep understanding of his past, his present feelings, his thoughts and will. It requires a knowledge of the psychological makeup of man as well as the discernment of the Holy Spirit to assist in this ministry.

The seat of man's personality is his soul. It is his soul that presents him as a rational, affectionate and wilful being. It is the soul that enables the person to relate, feel, reason, imagine, soul-search, remember, etc. Spiritually unregenerated, it remains earth bound.

The natural man lives a soul-body existence. His body functions as directed by the soul. His thoughts, his emotions, his decisions determine the movements of the body. His spirit, not yet touched by the Spirit of God, has no control of the soul and as such works independently of the Spirit. Because his existence is soulish, his desires are earthbound. The result is his tendency to move in the direction of *sarx*.

The Flesh or 'Sarx'

The Greek word *sarx* is translated in the English language as 'flesh'. In the literal sense, *sarx* refers to the human body (2 Corinthians 10:3a; Galatians 2:20; Philippians 1:22). However in a more figurative sense, *sarx* refers to man in his weakness (Romans 6:19, 8:3).[5] It is the seat of all sinful activity.[6]

Sarx is the evil principle that opposes God. Since it opposes God, it becomes a tool of Satan. When a person allows *sarx* to dominate his being, he is also allowing Satan a foothold in his life. Consequently, one of the goals of Christian counselling is to deliver the counsellee from the control of *sarx* into the freedom of the Spirit.

In Galatians 5, Paul discusses the Spirit-flesh dichotomy. He says,

16 *But I say, walk by the Spirit, and you will not carry out the desires of the flesh.*
17 *For the flesh sets its desire against the Spirit, and the Spirit against the flesh; for these are in opposition to one another, so that you may not do the things that you please.*

18 *But if you are led by the Spirit, you are not under the Law.*

19 *Now the deeds of the flesh are evident, which are: immorality, impurity, sensuality,*

20 *idolatry, sorcery, enmities, strife, jealousy, outbursts of anger, disputes, dissensions, factions,*

21 *envying, drunkenness, carousing, and things like these, of which I forewarn you that those who practice such things shall not inherit the kingdom of God.*

These flesh-oriented activities prevent a person from inheriting the kingdom of God. It prevents a person from experiencing wholness of body, soul and spirit. Because it is earthward and fleshly, it is opposed to all that is heavenward and holy. The natural orientation of *sarx* is towards sin and Paul clearly makes this plain in his discussion in Romans 7:

14 *For we know that the Law is spiritual; but I am of flesh, sold into bondage of sin.*

15 *For that which I am doing, I do not understand; for I am not practising what I would like to do, but I am doing the very thing I hate.*

16 *But if I do the very thing I do not wish to do, I agree with the Law, confessing that it is good.*

17 *So now, no longer am I the one doing it, but sin which indwells me.*

18 *For I know that nothing good dwells in me, that is, in my flesh; for the wishing is present in me but the doing of the good is not.*

19 *For the good that I wish, I do not do; but I practise the very evil that I do not wish.*

20 *But I am doing the very thing I do not wish, I am no longer the one doing it, but sin which dwells in me.*

21 *I find then the principle that evil is present in me, the one who wishes to do good.*

> ²² *For I joyfully concur with the law of God in the inner man,*
> ²³ *but I see a different law in the members of my body waging war against the law of my mind, and making me a prisoner of the law of sin which is in my members.*
> ²⁴ *Wretched man that I am! Who will set me free from the body of this death?*
> ²⁵ *Thanks be to God through Jesus Christ our Lord! So then, on the one hand I myself with my mind am serving the law of God, but on the other, with my flesh the law of sin.*

It is apparent from Romans 7 that the natural tendency of man is to do the opposite of what his mind is telling him. He knows what is right and proper, but he does not do what he ought to do. Instead of following the dictates of the mind, man follows the dictates of his flesh. The only way out of this predicament is Jesus Christ (Romans 7:25). It is only Jesus who can deliver a person from the hold of *sarx* and usher him into a life in the Spirit.

Until we are willing daily to allow Christ to be Lord and to submit to His will and Word, our souls will run our lives. As Frost puts it, 'Divorced from the releasing power of the Holy Spirit, man is a mind-bound, time-bound, earthbound, two-dimensional creature – falling far short of the freedom for which he was originally created'.[7]

Spirit

The spirit is that part of man that is capable of responding to divine influences (Romans 8:16). It is that part of man that can respond in worship to God, to communicate in fellowship with Him and obey Him. It is that part of man that will not rest until it finds rest in God through Christ. Apart from the renewing work of the Holy Spirit, man is spiritually lifeless. He is spiritually dead; dead in his trespasses and sin (Ephesians 2:1–3). This is the condition of the natural man when the spirit within him is inactive. As the Apostle Paul puts it, *'a natural man does not accept the things of the Spirit of God; for they are foolishness to him, and he cannot understand them, because they are spiritually appraised'* (1 Corinthians 2:14). The natural man cannot respond to God in spirit because he is not yet spiritually alive. For this reason, Jesus says we must be born again (John 3:1–3).

The Human Spirit made Alive at Conversion

At conversion, the spirit of man is made alive by the Holy Spirit. He is able to communicate with God and relate to Him because he is made spiritually alive. He knows that he is a child of God because the Holy Spirit bears witness with his spirit that he is a child of God (Romans 8:16). It is this experience of the renewal of the spirit that distinguishes the Christian from the not-yet-Christian. For the Christian, his *pneuma* or spirit must be dominated by the Spirit of God. This renewed spirit engages in spiritual witness and warfare, and becomes the faculty of spiritual discernment.[8]

We become spiritually vibrant and attuned to God when we are made alive by the Spirit of God. When a person is born again, the soul comes under the influence of the Holy Spirit working through the human spirit. We are energised by the Spirit of God who fills us and enables us to receive divine revelation. Our spirit is strengthened by the Holy Spirit, and our prayer and worship take on new meaning as we enter into an intimate communion with God. Jesus says, *'God is spirit, and those who worship Him must worship in spirit and truth'* (John 4:24). The enlivened spirit of man can respond to the Spirit of God and experience a worship that is deep and meaningful.

The Sanctified Mind

The human spirit energised by the Holy Spirit can be a powerful instrument of God's love and grace. When our spirit is made alive, our soul can be sanctified. When our soul is sanctified, the resultant product is a sanctified mind, a sanctified heart, a sanctified conscience and a sanctified will. This is the state of a man who is baptized in the Holy Spirit.

A sanctified mind is opposed to the 'mind of the flesh' or the 'sensuous mind' that Paul talks about (Colossians 2:18). The Greek word for mind is *nous*. *Nous* as Guthrie puts it is not in itself good or bad. Its moral standing is determined by what is dominating it, either the Holy Spirit or the flesh.[9] Guthrie further says,

> 'When the mind does not acknowledge God, it becomes base (*adokimos*), a state which leads to improper conduct (Romans 1:28). Paul dares to say that God gave men up to such a mind. This seems to mean that refusal to acknowledge God has an adverse effect, which makes it harder for the mind to receive subsequent revelations of God. Elsewhere, when Paul speaks of the minds of unbelievers, he maintains that they have been blinded by Satan (2 Corinthians 4:4). Yet for believers the mind is not only enlightened (2 Corinthians 4:6), but can be renewed (Romans 12:2).[10]

Paul in other passages talks about the need of man to have the mind of God (Romans 11:34). A sanctified mind is a mind that is conformed to the mind of God (1 Corinthians 2:16). The mind functions in its most wholesome form when it fulfils the will of God.

The problem with many Christians is that they allow the soul to dominate instead of submitting to God's spirit working through the human spirit. When the mind is not controlled by God it becomes the ground upon which Satan will sow his seeds of destruction. A disturbed mind is not Spirit-controlled. It is a mind exposed to the influence of demonic powers. Wholeness can be experienced when the mind is Spirit-controlled.

Meng asked for help because he was constantly tormented by terrifying nightmares. He was afraid of the dark after his mother's death and would break out into cold sweat with fear at nights. Meng has always loved the Lord and could not understand what was happening to him. As we led Meng to recall his past and as he relived the hurts and distress of childhood, he found a release in the Lord. However, the nightmares would still occasionally haunt him and he would relapse into deep fear. We suggested to Meng the necessity of filling his mind with the thoughts of Jesus and His love. As Meng began to think of the beauty of Jesus and meditate on God's Word, the mental images that tormented him disappeared. He related to us a dream of how he was once again attacked by a host of 'devils' and of how in his dream, he began to resist the 'devils' by citing Scripture. The dream ended in a fierce struggle between him and the 'devils'. He awoke that night knowing that he would not be disturbed by those nightmares again because he was clear in his mind that he had the victory of Christ.

The Sanctified Heart

Wholeness and health can also be experienced through a sanctified heart. Paul sees the heart as the place where faith is exercised (Romans 10:10). It is also the place where Christ dwells (Ephesians 3:17). The heart can be referred to as the centre of affection or the seat of emotions (2 Corinthians 2:4; 7:2; Philemon 7, 20). A sanctified heart is a heart of love. It is a heart influenced by the Holy Spirit and bearing His fruit of love and its consequential ramifications of joy, peace, patience, kindness, goodness, faithfulness, gentleness, and self-control (Galatians 5:22–23). It is a heart that seeks to please God and worship Him.

A sanctified heart is also a heart of compassion. It feels for others and seeks to help those in need. The heart of Jesus is a heart of compassion. It was always out of compassion that Jesus fed the hungry, performed His many miraculous acts and did His work of counselling. We believe it is also imperative for us as lay counsellors to have this same heart of compassion so that many will be blessed by our ministry and receive the comfort of the Lord.

When a person's heart is filled with anger, bitterness, hatred, strife, jealousy, impurity and the like, his soul is not in harmony with the Spirit. Deliverance from all these negative attributes are necessary for the wholeness of soul. Christian counselling seeks to make such a deliverance possible.

A Clear Conscience

Closely related to the realm of the emotions is the conscience. Part of the soul is the conscience. The conscience is the human barometer for right and wrong. It enables a person to make a judgement as to whether a rule or standard is violated. When a rule is in fact violated, a sense of guilt is produced as an inner condemnation of a wrong done.

All of us, Christians or not-yet-Christians, are endowed with a conscience. The Apostle indicates this in Romans 2:14–16,

> [14] *For when the Gentiles who do not have the Law do instinctively the things of the Law, these, not having the Law, are a law to themselves,*
> [15] *in that they show the work of the Law written in their hearts, their conscience bearing witness, and their thoughts alternatively accusing or else defending them,*
> [16] *on the day when, according to my gospel, God will judge the secrets of men through Christ Jesus.*

A person who is Spirit-filled will have a conscience that is sensitive to the influence of the Holy Spirit. The Holy Spirit through the conscience will produce a sense of conviction of sin when the Christian moves away from

God's path of righteousness. Failure to obey the Spirit results in a feeling of guilt. This sense of guilt however can be eradicated through the process of counselling where the counsellee is led to a point of repentance and reconciliation with God. A clear conscience is necessary for wholeness of mind and spirit.

The Sanctified Will

The Spirit-filled person not only has a sanctified mind, heart and conscience, but also a sanctified will. God has given to all of us the faculty of the will and we are given the right of choice. We are sovereign in so far as our will is concerned. But when our spirit is made alive by the Holy Spirit, we are also given the choice to surrender our wills to God as well. We are given the choice to allow God's will to prevail over our wills.

The path of the natural man is soulish in so far as the decision-making process is concerned because his dependence is on his mind and emotions. However, the spiritual man can be Spirit-guided when he allows the Holy Spirit to work through his spirit in order to influence his soul in making a decision that is Spirit-led. The spiritual man takes his reference point from Jesus who in His prayer in Gethsemane said, *'My Father, if it is possible, let this cup pass from Me; yet not as I will, but as Thou wilt'* (Matthew 26:39). A Spirit-filled person desires only to fulfil the will of God.

This, however, is not so for the natural man or the carnal Christian. His philosophy is 'My will be done regardless'. Man's attempt to assert his own will against the will of God has led him to all kinds of mental and emotional ills. However, as he is helped to submit his will to God's will, he can receive wholeness and health.

Christian counselling aims at the healing of the whole person. It is our prayer that through the process of Spirit-guided counselling many will be ministered to in their spirit, soul and body.

Chapter 5

An Integrative Approach

During the recession of 1987, Chen brought Lin to visit with me (Isaac) one Sunday morning after the service. Chen, a member of our church, had been counselling Lin for some time before they came to visit me. Lin who was a senior secretary in her company had been retrenched because the company was doing badly as a result of the recession. Owing to the retrenchment, Lin went through a bout of depression and it was during this time that Chen met her and ministered to her the comfort of Jesus. Through the initial ministry of Chen, Lin and her family accepted Christ as their Lord and Saviour.

That Sunday, Chen decided to bring Lin and her family to meet with me so that they could receive ministry. After the church service, Chen introduced me to Lin, her husband and their little son. As I spoke to Lin, I could feel the disappointment in her voice as she spoke about her retrenchment. Her fear was her inability to find a suitable job as she was now in her early forties. She could not bear the thought of having to stay at home after having worked all her life. That morning, I laid hands on Lin and prayed that the Lord would bring about a release of her fears, and God did it.

Chen continued to minister to Lin and introduced her to a small group. There Lin found acceptance in the fellowship of new friends. A few months later, Lin and her husband joined the baptism and membership class of the church in preparation for the baptism of her whole family.

In the meantime Lin went through many unsuccessful job interviews. These were moments of discouragement, but Lin learned to trust in the Lord. After several months of unsuccessful interviews, Lin was offered a second interview in a large multi-national corporation just a week before her baptism. She had asked me to remember her in prayer as she prepared for the second interview.

On the day of her baptism, she came early to see me. With her face beaming with joy, she told me that God had answered her prayer. She had come early in order that I could spend some time in prayer with her to give thanks to God for His love and goodness. It was indeed a moment of joy and victory.

Lin had received ministry, not only from Chen and me, but also from the small group and the church as a whole. She not only found release from her depression and a job that she needed, but she had found for herself Christ, the Counsellor of counsellors, and a community that cared.

Several factors assisted Lin's release from depression. Firstly, she had the benefit of ministry from Chen who took time to counsel with her and share as a friend. Secondly, she had the benefit of her pastor who would intermittently counsel with her. Thirdly, she had the benefit of the small group which provided support and fellowship. Fourthly, she had the benefit of the church as the caring community which in many ways made her and her family feel accepted as new members of the community. There was in this ministry a working together of various component parts of the church with one single motive, and that is, the restoration of Lin to wholeness and healing.

The above approach in counselling is what we call an **integrative approach**. Various component parts of the church are called in to assist in the ministry of counselling. The integrative approach uses all available church-based resources to assist in the healing process.

The Body of Christ, we believe, has the God-appointed task of bringing comfort, restoration and healing to God's people. This is to be done in tandem with the helping and counselling efforts of secular institutions and bodies. Whilst doctors, psychiatrists, social workers and others in such helping professions in society play significant roles in providing professional care and counselling, there remains a gap in terms of support networks and follow-through facilities that the Christian community can provide for the Christian and those open to the influence of the Christian faith.

It has been our privilege to work with psychiatrists and doctors in the community to whom or from whom persons needing help have been referred. We consider this link-up essential. Whilst it is ideal to have Christian doctors, psychiatrists, social workers, lawyers and other Christian professionals within the Church, other professional persons in society may also be consulted should the need arise. We see professionals as fulfilling a role that is specialised and irreplaceable and complementary to the role of the Church in people helping. It has been an encouraging experience for us to find persons in the helping professions responding to God's call of a togetherness in Christian outreach to the needy. A prominent Christian doctor who attended one of our Counsellor Training sessions said, 'This course has given me an increased conviction that there is a need for counselling and that inadequate as I am, there is a place for me to serve.'

Church-based counselling not only provides an avenue for healing, but also a community to facilitate wholeness and growth. Church-based counselling allows for a system of accountability that will minimize irresponsible action. As counselling is related to the emotional well-being of the counsellee, it is essential that a system of accountability be devised so that proper supervision can be maintained to facilitate care and healing and proper integration be managed to expedite the goal.

The integrative approach to counselling has its context within the framework of the local church. Counsellees will be ministered to within a Christian environment and with methods that are biblical in orientation. Although Christian counselling is Church orientated, it is a ministry open to non-Christians as well. The very character of the Church as God's agent of reconciliation and peace compels the Church to be inclusive in her ministry. The church cannot be selective in her ministry of counselling. Her ministry transcends her membership. Consequently, in the work of counselling, we go beyond to all. We are called to minister to those within the Church as well as those outside the Church. The only condition is the counsellee's willingness to accept counselling that is based on scriptural principles.

To help us understand the dynamics of Christian counselling and the nature of the integrative approach, it is useful for us to look at a working definition of Christian counselling.

Christian Counselling Defined

Christian counselling can be defined as a ministry process where a counsellee finds help through an encounter with a Christian counsellor who in his capacity as a caring person, and in relation to his church as a caring community renders assistance with the goal of reducing emotional pain, giving direction, clearing doubts, affirming confidence, bringing comfort, changing attitudes and eventually directing the counsellee to faith in the Risen Christ who remains the Counsellor par excellence.

The above definition speaks of Christian counselling as a ministry process. Although the process begins with the Christian counsellor, his church stands with him as the caring community that will give all the assistance in the restoration of wholeness in spirit, soul and body.

The Christian counsellor serves as a partner in the ministry of wholeness within the context of the church.

There is a difference between Christian counselling and secular counselling. The difference between Christian counselling and secular counselling is its orientation and approach. The emphasis in Christian counselling is the adoption of biblical answers to human problems. It uses other social disciplines not as the main thrust in counselling, but as tools to augment the biblical approach to counselling.

Christian counselling is essentially a ministry to those who seek to find in Christ an answer to their needs. Gary Collins suggests that 'counselling might help counsellees recognise unconscious harmful attitudes, teach interpersonal skills and new behaviours, or show how to mobilise one's resources to face a crisis. At times, such counselling guided by the Holy Spirit, can free a counsellee from hang-ups which prevent him or her from growing to Christian maturity.'[1]

Christian counselling recognizes that the basic problem of man is sin. Sin separates man from God and the problem that man faces is a reflection of his inner condition. Christian counselling points to Christ as the answer to wholeness and healing. Yet God uses the agency of the human person to communicate this message of hope and wholeness.

The integrative approach to Christian counselling is like a partnership where members of a Caring Community join hands in bringing comfort, healing and wholeness to one in need. As defined above, there are three partners in this ministry process: **The Christian Counsellor, The Caring Community, and Christ Himself**.

The Christian Counsellor

Christian counselling remains the special domain of the Christian. A non-Christian cannot engage in Christian counselling because the central figure in Christian counselling is Christ Himself. Jesus is the source of all healing and wholeness. It is precisely for this reason that the Christian counsellor must be a Christian who knows Christ in a personal way and believes unequivocally that Christ is the answer to the needs of man.

Qualities of a Good Christian Counsellor

Christians who have a burden for helping others have often asked us what a good counsellor should be. Whilst we do not have definitive answers ourselves, we find general guidelines useful for the genuine seeker. We would like to highlight some of the basic qualities of a good Christian counsellor.

Firstly, he must love Jesus. A Christian counsellor needs to be committed in his service to the Master. In ministering to the counsellee, he does so as an expression of his love for Jesus. It is this expression of love and a desire to please Jesus that enables the counsellor to go a second mile in this ministry of inner healing. It is his love for Jesus that ushers the counsellee also into the presence of the Master and enables the counsellee to consider Jesus for himself. A love for Jesus always issues forth in dedicated service (John 21:16).

Secondly, a Christian counsellor must have a heart of compassion. A counsellor needs to reach out in the spirit of care and love. It was in the spirit of compassion that Jesus reached out and ministered to those in need (Matthew 9:36; 15:32). It was out of compassion that He fed the hungry and healed the sick. It is the same compassion that Jesus requires of us in the ministry of reconciliation, inner healing, deliverance and release. Whilst we abhor the sin and wickedness that may entrap the counsellee, there must be a compassionate desire to help the repentant.

Thirdly, the Christian counsellor must be a willing listener. Christian counsellors can minister effectively only when they understand the counsellee's dilemma. They are not to presume knowledge of the counsellee's problem without sufficient probing and listening. Christian counsellors must always remember that to determine a counsellee's problem without listening sufficiently to the counsellee is to be irresponsible as a counsellor. Christian counsellors should be patient in listening and try as far as possible to be accurate in the understanding of the issue. Perceptive listening is the hallmark of a good Christian counsellor as it is through effective listening that the counsellor can empathise with the counsellee and discern his needs.

Fourthly, the Christian counsellor must be willing to work under authority. When ministering within the context of the church, the counsellor must be willing to place himself under the authority of the senior Pastor or the person in charge of counselling. Lay counsellors should keep the relevant authority informed about counsellees and discuss some of the problems they may have with them, within the framework of confidentiality, of course.

Fifthly, the Christian counsellor must be willing to work hand in hand with other members of the Body. Counselling is not a one-man show. The counsellor must recognize that the goal of counselling is not to glorify himself, but to minister to the one who is going through a difficult phase in his life. There may be other members of the church who could give better assistance. If this is the case, the counsellor should not be hesitant in seeking the aid of others in the counselling process.

Sixthly, the Christian counsellor must be a person of prayer. It is necessary to augment counselling with prayer. As we minister to the counsellee, we also need divine wisdom in the handling of each situation. Therefore, we need constantly to turn to God for guidance and assistance in the handling of each counsellee.

Whilst all Christians are challenged to be involved in the ministry of counselling, the reality of the situation is that not all are endowed with the gift of counselling. Nonetheless, it pays for every Christian to have some knowledge of Christian counselling so that he can be of some assistance when the need arises to assist in the ministry of wholeness and inner healing.

Generally speaking, it is useful to classify Christian counsellors within a particular parish into two categories. The first is the Counselling Elder and the second, the Lay Christian Counsellor.

The Counselling Elder

Counselling Elders are those who have been appointed by the Senior Pastor (or Church Elder) to co-ordinate the work of counselling and the training of counsellors in a particular parish. These persons have a special gift in counselling and may be working full-time as a pastor or lay ministry staff, or he may be a lay person appointed to do the work of co-ordination and training. The Counselling Elders are responsible to the Senior Pastor (or counsellor in charge) for the smooth running of the counselling ministry of the church.

The Lay Christian Counsellor

The Lay Christian Counsellor would normally be the Church member who is interested in the ministry of care and comfort and who avails himself or herself, to be equipped for the ministry of counselling.

It is our prayer that more and more Christians would consider such a ministry and avail themselves for training. It is precisely for this reason that this book has been written. The main burden is to encourage lay persons to express their Christian commitment through the ministry of care and counselling.

Through our experience in the parish, we have noticed that some members of the congregation have a gift and propensity to counsel more than others. Because they are approachable, compassionate and endowed with the ability to empathise with others, their friends naturally turn to them when they need a listening ear. The vibrance of Christ's work in these Christians mark them out as persons to whom others would go for Christian counsel. As such, members are encouraged to exercise their gifts in the context of a church based ministry. In this way the Church can express a corporate ministry of Christian counselling that is extensive and outreaching. There is therefore a need for 'training' in the articulation of a co-ordinated effort in Christian counselling. It is precisely for this reason that we have exposed members of our church to be trained in the basics of Christian counselling and the specially gifted ones to more intense involvement in the counselling ministry.

The need for a greater number of lay counsellors is evident. Whilst there are those who are fortunate in having friends to turn to for counselling, there are others who may not enjoy the same privilege. In fact, few have the privilege of contact with supportive friends who would minister to their needs.

Accountability

The counselling ministry is best looked at conceptually not only as an individual effort but as a supportive network. This is because, like other Church ministries such as evangelism, missions and social outreach, counselling is a body ministry and not only does the counsellee need a receiving and nurturing community within which to grow and develop, the counsellor too needs such a support and resource as well.

Part of the educative mission of the Church is to equip Christians who are called to a caring and supportive ministry, so that they can be effective one-to-one counsellors working within the supportive network of the church. Just as a missionary is sent by the Church as its ambassador carrying the good news of our Lord, so the counsellor is one who represents the caring concern of the Body of Christ. As such, the counsellor is also accountable to the spiritual leader of the Church, which in most cases is the Senior Pastor, Associate Pastor, Church Elder or the full-time or specially appointed person in charge of counselling.

While many Christians may not feel adequate or inclined to minister to persons with needs, they can be challenged to be involved as caring members in support groups within which counsellees can receive comfort, fellowship and Christian love. Such fellowship and nurture groups may be on-going Church or Christian groups or may be specially-formed groups with the specific aim of nurturing spiritual growth and maturity. These groups operate within the caring community which is the Church.

In our experience we have found lay counsellors playing a very effective role when working alongside the Pastor or counselling Elders. In this way they not only acquire skills, but come under constant supervision. They not only provide help but through this process are also helped to become better counsellors.

Lay counselling however becomes a problem if a counsellee becomes overdependent on a counsellor. Just remaining at the personal friendship level in counselling may lead to a personal dependence of the counsellee on the counsellor if the counselling period becomes excessively prolonged. The counsellee may in fact be excluding himself from fellowship with others who can provide a caring fellowship and expedite the healing process. It is precisely for this reason that the Lay counsellor needs to work alongside the Pastor or counselling Elder and the Caring Community so that the counsellee can benefit from the care of the Body. This leads us to the second partner in the ministry process called the Caring Community.

The Caring Community

We have seen that the ministry of counselling and healing is an integral function of the church. Right from the very outset, the Church existed as a healing and caring community.

The coming of the Holy Spirit at Pentecost not only brought about a caring and healing community but it also resulted in persons within the Christian community being endowed with a variety of spiritual gifts. As the Apostle Paul puts it, *'He gave some as apostles, some as prophets, some as evangelists, and some as pastors and teachers, for the equipping of the saints for the work of service, to the building up of the body of Christ'* (Ephesians 4:11–12).

It should be noted that the apostles, the prophets, the evangelists, pastors and teachers were all lay persons in those days. There was no distinction between the laity and clergy. Everyone was a lay person but endowed with gifts for the work of service and the building up of the body of Christ.

Although the gifts are many, it is the Holy Spirit who distributes the gifts *'to each one individually just as He wills'*. That is to say, some are possessed with gifts that enable them to serve in frontal work in the counselling ministry, while others are given gifts that are of a more supportive nature.

The endowment of gifts upon God's people allows the creation of a community where people in need can receive counsel from a counsellor as well as support from a caring community. There is within the church, the counsellor as well as the Caring Community. The counsellors are those who are engaged in the person-to-person counselling situation. These are those who are endowed with counselling gifts. Then there is the Caring Community. It consists of all those endowed with the variety of supportive gifts as elaborated in 1 Corinthians 12 and Romans 12. Thus, when a person turns to the church for counselling, he has not only the support of the counsellor, but also the support of the Caring Community. There is here a support system that allows a follow-up of all counsellees to receive ministry not only from the counsellor but also from the Caring Community.

Caring Groups

The Caring Community consists of individual church members as well as caring groups of selected persons who are appointed to assist a particular counsellee and to see him through his period of distress. Caring groups can consist of Bible Study groups, Fellowship groups as well as the Small Groups. These assist in providing support and fellowship to the counsellees.

Whilst the Caring Group can be made up of selected church members, the Caring Community is made up of the Church as a whole. It includes every Christian who has been called to minister God's love; it includes all who desire to minister God's word of compassion, peace and hope. It includes those with an inclination to counsel as well as those without an inclination to counsel. Those who are not inclined to counsel, can provide the community support that will assist a counsellee in his recovery process. The Caring Community provides the therapeutic context in which the counsellee receives the emotional support that would enable him to go through his crisis period.

Meier, Minirth and Wichern, in their book *Introduction to Psychology and Counselling*, suggested that, 'although the emphasis in Christian counselling is on the relationship of two individuals, the counsellor and counsellee, a larger fellowship is in the background.'[2] William Backus, a Christian psychologist and associate pastor of a large Lutheran church in Minnesota, wrote these words: 'I believe counselling belongs in the Church and that psychologists and psychiatrists should play the role of assistants to the Body of Christ in healing emotional disorder.' He goes on to say that, 'lay Christians too may have counselling ministries in the church. Good order and the welfare of counsellees require that they perform their ministries under the direction of the pastor and his assistants and yokefellows.'[3]

When the church functions as a Caring Community, the

senior Pastor (or Church Elder/Leader) needs to exercise his God-given authority to co-ordinate the ministry. His authority must be respected by all Christian counsellors as long as they are members of the said church and operate within the jurisdiction of the said minister or elder. The senior Pastor serves as the senior Executive in the ministry of counselling. It is his responsibility to train his counsellors or engage reliable counsellor trainers to assist him in the training. Experienced Counselling Elders can also be appointed as counsellor trainers. Pastoral leadership and interest in counselling is therefore important if a ministry of counselling within a church is to succeed.

The Christian Friend

Within the Caring Community is also what we would like to call the Christian Friend. The Christian Friend may be a member of the Caring Group or a member of the Church who has been chosen to assist a counsellee in his recovery process. The Christian Friend need not be a counsellor, but a caring person who desires to assist the Lay Counsellor in his ministry to troubled people. The Christian Friend is one to whom the Christian counsellor can call upon for additional support to the counsellee in the ministry of befriending.

The Counselling Team

Sometimes it may be necessary to handle a counselling case, not as a single counsellor, but as a Counselling Team. The Team could consist of the Pastor, the Counselling Elder, the Lay Counsellor, the Christian Friend, and some members of the Caring Group. The size of the group can vary, but this provides a wider caring circle to whom a counsellee can turn to should he be in special need. This is most helpful when a Christian counsellor is counselling a counsellee with suicidal tendencies. In circumstances like this, he may want to widen the membership of his team to include medical doctors, psychologists, psychiatrists or those in other helping professions.

A Framework of Confidentiality

The question in some of your minds at this juncture may be: If so many people are involved in this caring ministry, how then can confidentiality be preserved?

This is a tricky situation but not without a solution. Two things should be noted. First of all, not all counsellees need community support of the same intensity. In some cases the ministry of a lay counsellor alone would suffice as the counsellee may already be a part of a caring fellowship. Secondly, in situations where community support is needed for the counsellee, a Counselling Team would first be involved in the counselling process. A member of a Caring Group would also be a member of the Counselling Team. It is only when the counsellee has gained confidence in the Counselling Team and the counsellor from the Caring Group that the counsellor is introduced to the Caring Group. In this instance, it is unnecessary for members of the Caring Group to know the problem of the counsellee as the responsibility of ministry and caring would be that of the lay counsellor from the Group. The responsibility of the Caring Group is to be supportive. It should be noted that the Caring Group could be in the form of a small group, a Fellowship group or a Bible Study group.

Christ, the Counsellor Par Excellence

Christian counselling is not complete without the counsellor leading the counsellee to the person of Jesus, the Counsellor par excellence, and the third and most important person in the partnership. Counselling is Christian not only because it is done by a Christian counsellor but because the Christian who does the counselling recognises that it is Jesus who ultimately brings grace and peace in fullest measure. Although this is the philosophy, counsellees must never be coerced by Christian counsellors into accepting Jesus as Lord. Counsellors need to be sensitive to the readiness of the counsellee to receive the Gospel and should never attempt to force on them a decision. At the same time, the Christian counsellor should never play down the fact that the best help they can ultimately offer to the counsellee is abundant life in Christ Jesus.

Jesus says, *'I am the light of the world'*. When Jesus the Light comes into the life of a counsellee, He reveals the truth about the counsellee's situation, and helps him along the path of restoration. But Jesus is not only the Light. He is also the Way, the Truth and the Life. He is the Way to God; He is the Way to healing and wholeness; He is the Way to release and freedom. When a person is lost in the journey of life, he is brought back into the path of wholeness and healing through the person of Jesus.

Jesus is also the Truth. It is when we know the truth about ourselves that the process of healing within begins. The truth sets us free. Jesus desires each one of us to know the truth about ourselves; He wants us to know that we can be cleansed and healed from our past hurts and pains; He wants us to know that we can grow in maturity when we accept the truth about life and eternity.

Christ is the cement that binds the work of the component parts of the caring community. He is the one who brings to completion the work of inner healing. He is the one who makes complete the Integrative Approach to a ministry of counselling.

Jesus is the Life. He brings freshness to life; He rejuvenates a burnt-out life and gives it a new lease; He restores a tired spirit and makes it alive again; He resurrects the spiritually lifeless and gives them an amazing vibrance. He makes a counsellee whole and revitalized for service.

Chapter 6

A Ministry of Inner Healing

A pastor of an American church said with tears in his eyes, 'I'm so glad God sent you across the miles to pass this way. I've been needing to talk to someone about my feelings for a long time.' This pastor, a God-fearing servant of the Lord, began to share with us the deep hurts he and his wife sustained in leading a church of parishioners who were unsympathetic to evangelistic outreach, who didn't want to consider any suggestions for church growth and wanted only to maintain the status quo. As the pastor poured out his frustrations that had been bottled up for a long time, he was sad that he had reached a point of defeat. He was going to give it all up and leave the ministry. As he spoke, cried and poured out thoughts suppressed for years, he found a release and renewed strength to go on waiting on the Lord.

There are two important concepts embodied in this experience. The first concept is that everyone needs the ministry of inner healing, even men set apart to serve God. The second is that we need to be open and honest with God regarding how we feel about our situations. We may not be able to find a compassionate counsellor who is able to bring us before the presence of God but we still need to go to God our Master Counsellor, to receive inner healing, comfort and renewal.

Pain and Suffering Come to All

Conflict is part and parcel of human life. The Christian is not exempt from hurts, pain and emotional stress. Being distressed, troubled and afflicted is not sin. It is when we dwell on the emotional disturbances and allow them to overwhelm us that we sin. The Christian needs to know and continually experience the power of God ministering to his personal needs. John Sandford in his book *The Transformation of the Inner Man* testifies to the healing of personal hurts, fears and conflicts. The point is that the continual process of inner healing is the privilege of the Christian who should not be ashamed that he needs it. Although the Christian may have psychological conflicts and the accompanying emotional symptoms like everyone else, the difference is that he has access to inner healing that comes from God, for restoration and renewal.

Paul constantly mentions the afflictions that are part of his ministry (Philippians 4:11–14) and goes on to mention the strength that Christ gives that is all-sufficient. It will be a mistake therefore to assume that Christians are immune to suffering and stress because Jesus tells us, *'In the world you have tribulation, but take courage; I have overcome the world'* (John 16:33).

We need not be afraid of the hurts and knocks in life because Jesus gives us strength to overcome them. We need not live under an illusion that as Christians we should not be affected by stress, and therefore attempt to hide from ourselves and others the fact that we are affected. Paul mentions the emotional stretching and turbulence that are part of his ministry in 2 Corinthians 6:4, 5 when he wrote, *'...but in everything commending ourselves as servants of God, in much endurance, in afflictions, in hardships, in distresses, in beatings, in imprisonments, in tumult, in labors, in sleeplessness, in hunger,...'* Those of us who love the Lord and seek to live in obedience to His service must be ready for the wounds and bruises from warfare against Satan and his cohorts.

Jesus Himself Suffered

Jesus Himself was troubled by conflicts as He ministered on earth. When Jesus saw Mary and the Jews crying over Lazarus' death, it is recorded that Jesus *'was deeply moved in spirit, and was troubled'* (John 11:33). In His own situation, Jesus expressed his conflicts as He bore the sin of man on Himself by saying, *'Now My soul has become troubled; and what shall I say, "Father, save Me from this hour?" But for this purpose I came to this hour.'* The agony of Christ's dying on the Cross was not only one of physical suffering but one of psychological torment as well. Jesus abhorred the thought of momentary separation from God as He bore the sin of mankind, but His goal was also to obey God the Father. In the Garden of Gethsemane, Jesus laboured in prayer as he grappled with this conflict and resolved it saying, *'My Father, if it is possible, let this cup pass from Me; yet not as I will, but as Thou wilt'* (Matthew 26:39). Jesus openly shared his feelings with 'Peter and the two sons of Zebedee', saying, *'My soul is deeply grieved, to the point of death; remain here and keep watch with Me.'* Jesus opened up Himself to allow Peter, James and John to empathise with him, yet the disciples, in their inability to appreciate the extent of His agony, fell asleep and could not keep watch with Him for one hour. So deep was Christ's agony that *'He was praying very fervently; and His sweat became like drops of blood, falling down upon the ground'* (Luke 22:44).

The Master's invitation to watch with Him is still open today. The call to all Christians is to be supportive to their agonising brethren in their hour of need. We need to remember that the marvellous privilege of ministering to our Lord in fact lies in our ministry to those in need.

Victory Over Conflicts

When Jesus found his disciples sleeping, he said to them, *'Why are you sleeping? Rise and pray that you may not enter into temptation'* (Luke 22:46). We need to be awake, alert, watchful and prayerful, not only over the needs of others but also over our own needs. We need to mutually minister one to another as we face conflicts in our sojourn on this earth. The Christian is not free from conflicts, trials and tribulations but he has victory over them in Christ Jesus. In fact, the Christian faces a greater conflict than the non-Christian because very often the goals of the Holy Spirit may be in direct conflict with the desires of the flesh. Paul puts it this way in Galatians 5:17, *'For the flesh sets its desire against the Spirit, and the Spirit against the flesh; for these are in opposition to one another, so that you may not do the things that you please.'* Often in exasperation over his own fleshly impediments, Paul exclaims, *'Wretched man that I am! Who will set me free from the body of this death?'* (Romans 7:24). However, Paul never allows this conflict to hamper his ministry as he continues to affirm that the answer to all these problems is Jesus when He wrote, *'Thanks be to God through Jesus Christ our Lord!'* (Romans 7:25).

Hence it is clear in Scripture that as long as man is in the flesh there will be the experience of conflict and internal strife. The Christian must not fall into the trap of believing he can avoid conflicts in this earthly life. This kind of reasoning causes the Christian to crumble in the face of conflict, and, instead of dealing with it in the Presence of the Lord, begin to sweep it aside and suppress it.

A Christian lady who has a son studying abroad kept herself very busy singing in a church choir, joining in all the senior citizens' activities and leading home Bible study groups. She was initially feeling very lonely and depressed when her son left her for studies overseas and felt it was silly of her even to feel that way. As a result, she immersed herself in activity and swept her feelings of deep hurt aside. One day, she collapsed in the middle of a function with high blood pressure and lost her memory of past events. As we counselled with her and led her to recall her past, the first thing she remembered was her anguish over her son's departure and her fear of losing him. From there the events of the past flowed back and she remembered how she felt rejected as a child, her father having died when she was very young. This vibrant and capable Christian lady recovered very quickly as she received inner healing from the Lord.

We need to learn to recognise our internal conflicts and bring them before our Lord without attempting to hide or conceal from Him, or try to deny they exist. All too often we may suppress our feelings and reactions, thinking that they have receded safely into our sub-conscious. This does not mean however that they have disappeared. Suppressed conflicts lead to damage within.

Redemptive Healing

Healing of the inner person begins first with the redemption and healing of the soul. We call this Redemptive Healing. It has to do with Christ's redemptive work on the cross. Through His death on the cross Christ has redeemed the sinner from the hold of Satan into the joy of His marvellous light (1 Peter 2:9).

Redemptive healing is the experience of conversion. It enshrines the words of Paul who said, *'Therefore if any man is in Christ, he is a new creature; the old things passed away, behold new things have come'* (2 Corinthians 5:17). Redemptive healing, as such, restores a sinner's relationship with God and enables a further work of healing to take place as we are moulded into the image of His Son.

David, a young man, still hovering between adolescence and adulthood, found himself faced with a series of problems. From a very young age, he had watched his father beat up his mother and he would often plead with him in hysteria to stop. On one occasion when he saw that his father was working up a temper and knowing the usual run of events would lead to aggression, he sneaked out of the house to call in the police. He made up a story that his father was attacking his mother with a knife and the police came with him. To his surprise when he came home with the policeman, his made-up tale was enacted before his eyes. His father had indeed threatened to slash his mother to death and the police immediately arrested him.

David had succeeded getting his father into prison only to find himself landed with the problem of supporting his entire family of five. He was a bitter and angry youth. He resorted to lying, cheating, borrowing and when all failed, tried to take his own life. He entered into deep depression and was bemoaning his situation. After repeated attempts at suicide, he was referred to a psychiatrist. He was also directed to the church for help. David found some friends in church who really cared for him. They listened to him and counselled with him. They helped him find a job that he liked and encouraged him to work hard at it. In his own words, he said, 'I've never been loved like that before!' As David fellowshipped with his new found friends who loved Jesus, he soon became interested in the Jesus whom they loved. His friends prayed and counselled with him, and introduced him to their Bible study group. Eventually, he accepted Jesus as his personal Saviour and Lord. As Christ worked in his life, he was free from the satanic grips of depression and experienced a Redemptive Healing in his life that changed him completely. He became more positive and was willing to allow God to work in other areas of his life such as his anger at his father. David found Redemptive Healing when he was introduced to the Person of Jesus. He found new life and strength in the Lord to face the problems he had.

While it is important to help a counsellee deal with the problem at hand in a practical way, it is also important to allow the counsellee the opportunity to see the love of

Jesus that is available for him or her as well. This is not to say that one should thrust the gospel of salvation down a counsellee's throat, so to speak. The whole attitude of sharing the gospel should be one of love and understanding as our God Himself gave man a choice of whether to accept or reject Him. The basic premise is that it is only in Christ that there can be healing that is complete, as He ministers to man's body, spirit and soul. Hence in ministry to the non-Christian, evangelism is the ultimate goal of Christian Counselling. As such, it is often necessary to allow a counsellee time to experience the grace of the Lord.

It should be noted that the freedom of the counsellee to make a personal choice must be honoured. There is a need to be patient and not push when hearts are not ready to receive Christ. We can continue to minister to someone who is not ready to receive Christ by giving him support in every way possible. We can make it clear that there is the avenue for complete and total healing in the redemptive blood of Jesus. We need to offer the Gospel of Salvation because, very often, when the counsellee is led to look at Jesus instead of merely focusing on his problems, the Light of Christ brings new hope and dispels darkness. The Gospel of Christ not only offers salvation for the soul of man but also brings about healing. It is interesting to recall that the word 'save' means in the original 'to heal' just as much as it does 'to rescue'.

Transformation Healing

While the non-Christian can be introduced to redemptive healing in Christ, the Christian can experience inner healing as an essential part of the transforming work of God in his life. Although Christians are 'new creatures' when they come into the saving knowledge of Jesus as their Lord and Saviour, the work of transformation in them is not yet complete. In fact, it has just begun. Sandford

107

explains that 'transformation is that process of death and rebirth whereby what was our weakness becomes our strength.'[1] At the point of our acceptance of Christ, we are made 'new' in the sense that we are enabled to see and realise our need for repentance and receive the gift of salvation in Jesus Christ. This does not mean that we instantly become perfect and are free from all the inclinations of our carnal personalities. Becoming *'new creatures'* and the fact that *'old things have passed away'* (2 Corinthians 5:17) refers to our status as children of God. We are in a position through the grace of Christ to be freed from the bondage of sin as we exercise faith. We have a right to freedom and release as heirs of God. We begin the process of transformation into which the blood of Christ has initiated us.

Renewal of Mind and Heart

The Christian grows as he studies the Word of God and attempts by the Holy Spirit to live by faith and obedience. This is an important aspect of Christian growth and we need continually to be *'transformed by the renewing of your mind'* (Romans 12:2), so that we may know the mind of God. Believing in the renewing of the mind is an important first step but it must be accompanied by a believing heart. In Romans 10:6–10 we are told that the righteousness based on faith has to do with the **heart**. Verse 10 reminds us that *'with the **heart** man believes'*. There is a difference between believing with the mind and believing with the heart.

Belief that comes from the very depths of our hearts is often the result of a deep work that God has done in our lives. This involves a breaking away from self and self-centred concerns so that the process of transformation can take its course. God often allows us to go through suffering so as to bring us to maturity. The path to glory is often preceded by the path of the Cross. Unless we are willing to tread the path of the Cross, we cannot walk the road of the Resurrection. Hence, 'Transformation proceeds by brokenness'.[2]

An accomplished businessman explained to us how he felt when he was retrenched after 30 years of striving to build up a company. It was a most unexpected downturn for him especially when his wife was then ill and he had just committed himself to buying a house. The trauma of losing his job at that late stage in life was therefore compounded by the domestic problems he had. He had been accustomed all his life to having things his way. This crisis broke him and he thought it was the end of the road for him. He began to reassess his life and having been a church-going Christian, he tried reaching out to God for the first time in his life.

He came to us for support and together we prayed and asked the Lord to reveal His will and plan for this dear brother. It was during this time that he wondered if he had really known God personally. He had never prayed to God from his heart and having been busy with business, golf and a demanding social life, he realised that he had in fact neglected his own wife and children. They had grown bitter over the years because of his non-involvement in their lives. He even discovered that he harboured a deep sense of inferiority that drove him to work relentlessly at success in his business. 'It's a strange thing,' he said to us, 'but though I've been so successful, I've deep down always felt inadequate because I don't have a degree.' There was a release, healing and comfort as the Lord ministered with him. At the end of a few months of intense personal anguish, he felt like a new person. His openness and desire to seek God at this time resulted in a life-transforming experience. He developed a confidence in the love of God and he said, 'It is because of this experience that I am now able to say like the Psalmist, *"I will fear no evil, thy rod and thy staff they comfort me."* I'm now a different person – I've finally learnt to love God.'

The miracle of transformation continued as this man,

having been reconciled with his family and with God, got another job and before long rose to the top of that corporation. Like Job, he had in fact much more than he had before. He was once again the successful man at the top. The difference was that he had been freed from the 'hang-up' – the inferiority he used to have that drove him to work so furiously at the expense of his family life. Transformation healing took place and he found God personal and real in his life so that not only would he love his wife and children as God desires, but he now spends his time serving the Lord through helping others.

Inner healing is God's work of redemption, restoration and renewal as he transforms man towards His perfection. For the Christian, the work of redemption through the blood of our Lord Jesus Christ has washed him clean and given him freedom from the penalty of sin. He needs to continue however, to allow God's work of transformation to heal the hurts and pains that come his way as he grows toward the likeness of the Lord.

The Need for Inner Healing

For many, emotional hurts and feelings have been blocked off deliberately from the mind and tucked into the subconscious. They remain in the subconscious and will surface at some time.

An analogy is appropriate here to explain the concept of such 'closed off' areas of our lives. In a house we once moved into, there was wet rot in some of the kitchen cabinets that had been festering for many years. In the night, the cockroaches from the drains outside would come into these infested areas and the stench that filled the kitchen told of their constant presence. These infested cabinets had been locked up and never opened for use and the simple solution recommended was to ignore these areas and use the rest of the large kitchen. As you can imagine, this hardly worked, for the pests moved outward, the cordoned off areas grew, and so did the stench. For health reasons we had to open up all the cabinets and clean out the pests, rot and foul odours. We battled with the vermin that were released and the cleansing finally came to an end. The closed closets were opened for good, and healthy living was finally possible.

Inner healing is something like that. It means the opening up of areas of our lives that have been locked up in the past, for the Holy Spirit to do a deep work of cleansing and restoration. Allowing the Holy Spirit to reveal to us areas of our lives that need to be dealt with is a prerequisite for inner healing.

Openness and Repentance Necessary

It is consistent with our sinful nature to hide from God; to think that we are good enough to go it on our own. It is like the Pharisee in the parable, who in his pride prayed, *'God, I thank Thee that I am not like all other people: swindlers, unjust, adulterers or even like this tax-gatherer. I fast twice a week; I pay tithes of all that I get'* (Luke 18:11, 12).

A distressed man once retorted to his wife, 'I don't need your God to help me – I've done things alone all my life and I'll continue to go on alone. I don't need love and charity or any one to care about me.' The bitterness and reaction of this young man resulted in a wall being built around him – a wall that has cut him off even from the healing power of Jesus. This young man is not only hurt, but he is proud.

The good news is that the love of Christ is able to penetrate the walls of resistance built up in this way. Our Good Lord forgives and comforts as people turn to him in repentance regardless of how rebellious they have been in the past. Hence, the love of Christ constrains us not to respond in reciprocal retaliation against such persons, but to love them and help them see the possible causes of their prejudices against the Church and God. More importantly, we need to help them come openly before God as those needing God's love and forgiveness.

Arrogant self-reliance is Satan's tool for keeping man away from experiencing personally the grace of our Lord. It is the way man tends to think. So-called 'self-made' persons find it hard to see the relevance of God in their lives. The focus is on personal achievement, status and rights. Before Paul's conversion he too was proud of his own status as *'a Hebrew of Hebrews'* (Philippians 3:5). But after his conversion, he saw himself as nothing when measured against the standards and magnificence of Christ. Paul proclaims, '...*it is no longer I who live, but Christ lives in me...*' (Galatians 2:20).

The recognition of one's sinful nature is a necessary first step towards inner healing. The holding on to a false sense of self-worth prevents man from seeing the grace of God. It is only as we come as undeserving sinners saved only by grace that the deep work of transformation can begin. Hence inner healing is a total renewal that begins with a deep conviction of sin. A person does not receive inner healing unless he allows the Holy Spirit to bring him to a point of total reliance on the grace of God and a deep conviction of his own worthlessness. To receive inner healing, a person should not trust in his own worth, but in his worth as a child of God, saved by grace through Christ.

Time Alone Does Not Heal

Paul says, *'Therefore, do not let sin reign in your mortal body that you should obey its lusts and do not go on presenting the members of your body to sin as instruments of unrighteousness...'* (Romans 6:12, 13). We need therefore to, *'cleanse ourselves from all defilement of flesh and spirit, perfecting holiness in the fear of God'* (2 Corinthians 7:1). We need to cast aside all encumbrances that weigh us down and which reduce our efficiency as servants of God.

To do this we need to honestly open ourselves before God and come to Him just as we are.

Some people keep emotions pent-up for years, or even a lifetime. A couple in their 60s had been married for the past 40 years or so. Jack was a sweet-natured and quiet man who was patient with Jill, a lively and outgoing wife. The couple seemed to have worked out a harmonious relationship with Jack minding his little Fiat car, and Jill enjoying her regular meetings with her lady friends. One day the equilibrium was completely upset. Over a tiff about a pail of water left in the garden after washing his car, Jack flew into a rage and flung the pail at his wife, narrowly missing her. He continued to hit her hard on her head over and over again until she ran for refuge into the house. How terrified she was as she faced her furious husband who had never before even raised his voice at her. He was caught up in a fury he himself could not understand, as he explained later. By some miracle, Jill managed to alert the neighbours to call the police and she was thankful that her life was spared as she recuperated in hospital. In the counselling sessions that ensued, Jack revealed his feelings of hurt in a series of happenings some 30 years ago. He had never spoken about his jealousy and anger at Jill, over her friendship with a mutual friend of theirs. He told himself that there was nothing wrong with Jill's friendship with this friend of his, but he would often seethe with anger as he watched Jill relate to him. He had kept this to himself for many years and he thought he had settled those feelings by letting time and age wash the hurts away. It did not happen that way. He was broken and shocked at what he did. He loved his wife and the last thing he wanted was to have anything happen to her. Tears of repentance flowed as he asked God for forgiveness and healing from wounds that had festered without his being aware that they were still there in the first place!

Shedding

It is important for us to deal with negative feelings and sin in our lives. In the ministry of inner healing, the conviction of sin mentioned earlier is followed by a choice as to whether a person is willing to be purged, in the sense of shedding or getting rid of known sin. It is the role of Christian counselling to bring about a willingness on the part of the counsellee to turn away from sin and allow God to make this possible. In the book of Daniel, in verse 10 of chapter 12, we read, *'Many will be purged, purified and refined; but the wicked will act wickedly, and none of the wicked will understand, but those who have insight will understand.'*

When a person wants to cling on to his sin and refuses to be purified and purged of it, he will not experience God's peace. The task of ministry is to help such persons receive the 'insight' that will enable them to understand that God loves them but abhors sin. Unless we are willing to move away from sin we are separating ourselves from God. Shedding of dead and infectious skin and tissues in a wound is a painful though necessary process in keeping the wound free from contamination, and expedite healing. In the same way, a willingness to shed sin and be free from it is a necessary step toward inner healing.

A middle-aged man came to us for ministry. He told us how he felt tormented by a deep sense of guilt as he attended Worship Services in his home church. He had a deep conviction of his sin. He had been secretly supporting a mistress for four years, and his wife who was a God-fearing lady did not know or suspect it. As he felt that God was showing him how loving his wife had been, despite his secret misdemeanour, he decided to break off the relationship with his mistress. It was a difficult decision for him because his mistress was also a loving and kind lady who demanded nothing for herself and was happy just to live in hiding from day to day. Hence he felt a responsibility to her as well. He sought the Lord and decided to seek counsel. As he received the counsel of God's Word, he was convinced that the severing of the relationship with his mistress was a necessary step in the right direction. He sought help for his mistress who did not take his decision well. She threatened suicide even though she was willing to receive counsel. It was a difficult counselling situation as this mistress felt victimised by a God who seemed to delight in taking everything she ever cared for from her. However, by a work of grace, during the period of counselling, this mistress found the love of Jesus real and personal and accepted the Lord Jesus in her life. On accepting the Lord, she found a new and fulfilled life in Christ, so much so that she was grateful to her lover for breaking the relationship in the first place.

This is but one example of the perfect grace of our Lord Jesus that works for good to those who love Him and are willing to put aside sin and be set right with the Master. Paul constantly reminds us that *'in order that the ministry be not discredited'* (2 Corinthians 6:3), we need to be always mindful of shedding known sin within us. He stresses the point that it is our humanness or affections that restrain and set back God's work in our lives (2 Corinthians 6:12).

Washing

As we open our hearts to God with a genuine conviction of sin, we can expect God to wash us clean of all unrighteousness and set us free. This is promised in Scripture as we read verses like Titus 3:3–6:

> ³ *For we also once were foolish ourselves, disobedient, deceived, enslaved to various lusts and pleasures, spending our life in malice and envy, hateful, hating one another.*
> ⁴ *But when the kindness of God our Saviour and His love for mankind appeared,*

> ⁵ *He saved us, not on the basis of deeds which we have done in righteousness, but according to His mercy, **by the washing of regeneration and renewing by the Holy Spirit,***
> ⁶ *whom He poured out upon us richly through Jesus Christ our Saviour...'*

Hence, we are told in verse 5 explicitly that it is not on the basis of what we have done or our righteousness but by washing of regeneration and renewing by the Holy Spirit. Just as physical wounds need to be washed, so do our wounded lives. Jesus says in John 13:8 to Peter that if he does not allow Him to wash his feet, then he will not be a part of Him – *'If I do not wash you, you have no part with Me.'* This symbolizes the need for all of us to be cleansed by Jesus. As we come to God the psalmist expresses so beautifully the sinner's sentiment in Psalm 51:1–4, which reads:

> ¹ *Be gracious to me, O God, according to Thy loving-kindness; according to the greatness of Thy compassion blot out my transgressions.*
> ² ***Wash me thoroughly from my iniquity, and cleanse me from my sin.***
> ³ *For I know my transgressions, and my sin is ever before me.*
> ⁴ *Against Thee, Thee only, I have sinned, and done what is evil in thy sight, so that Thou art justified when Thou dost speak, and blameless when Thou dost judge.'*

As we come in this way, we are forgiven and cleansed from all unrighteousness. Surely, though our sins be as scarlet, they will be white as snow. Jesus Himself assures us that He can wash us and we will be completely clean (John 13:10).

Receiving in faith this cleansing from our Lord is crucial

in inner healing. There are many who continue to suffer under the penalty of sin when they do not receive this truth of complete cleansing and renewal. A lady who was suffering from the guilt of having been a negligent mother in the past was not able to forgive herself for what she had done. Each time her errant son committed a wrongdoing, she would be tormented in her spirit. This resulted often in physical ailments as she continued to blame herself. It is not God's desire for us to be fettered by guilt but to come to Him in repentance, receive His forgiveness and be empowered henceforth to be obedient to His Word. The reminder in Scripture to us is that Jesus has paid the price for our redemption and we can be washed clean in the blood of the Lamb, however unworthy we are.

Just as the priests in the Old Testament washed at the Laver (Exodus 30:18–21) in preparation for their ministry at the altar in the Tabernacle, so too we, as a holy priesthood, have the facility to wash daily at the foot of the Cross and be cleansed for His ministry. Paul exhorts us with these words: *'Therefore, having these promises, beloved, let us cleanse ourselves from all defilement of flesh and spirit, perfecting holiness in the fear of God'* (2 Corinthians 7:1).

A dear Christian lady, Anna, has been touched by the Lord and released from alcoholism and habitual smoking. She loves the Lord dearly and is growing in her faith, witnessing to others over God's love. Her belief in the Lord is real and contagious and some of her friends have become interested in hearing about the love of Jesus. However, Anna used to feel depressed and would cry bitterly ever so often. The fact was that she did not feel worthy, clean nor deserving of God's love. I (Shirley) remember how Anna needed to 'unload' to someone the facts of her sordid past. She recounted to me how her father was a drunkard and how she was a victim of incest and sexual abuse. As she spoke, I could sense her mixed feelings and confusion of pain and relief. She said to me,

'You know, you don't even have to tell me that Jesus loves me because I've known that deep within me. The funny thing is that it's only now, right now that I can feel it as well as know it.'

The realisation of having been washed by the blood of Jesus can be real for us as we lay bare our lives and come honestly just as we are before the Lord. We certainly need to be open to God and dare to bare ourselves, our sins and our past before God so that the cleansing experience can be real. We can on our own go to God for cleansing and be washed clean by Him. We can also experience cleansing through the loving ministry of our pastor, elder, counsellor or godly friend. Ask them to pray with you and minister God's inner healing.

Will you do just that?

Chapter 7

A Ministry of Deliverance

Some years ago, a young lady was brought to church in a state of confusion. For a few days her parents had noticed her strange behaviour and wondered what was wrong with her. She was sent to her doctor but her doctor could not find anything medically wrong with her. At times she would appear coherent, but at other times she would appear quite incoherent and not in control of herself.

A member of our church happened to know the family and he suggested that Mary be sent to the church for counselling. Although Mary's family members were not Christians, they agreed to bring Mary to church because her state had worsened.

When Mary was brought to the church, she appeared fearful. As I (Isaac) counselled with her, she told me that she had felt something inexplicable take hold of her. She said that there were moments when a strange force would take over her vocal cords and speak. She could hear what was being said but was unable to control her speech. Her family doctor had told her parents that there were no apparent physiological reasons for her seizures.

As I spoke to her it became clear to me that Mary was demonized, and not wanting to frighten her I told her that Jesus could deliver her and release her if she would but accept Jesus as Lord. Mary had, before this episode, attended Christian meetings, and she understood her need to receive Christ if she was to be delivered. But before she could make a proper response, she began to manifest a strange behaviour. Instead of sitting in her chair, she became restless and began to crawl on the floor. It was at this juncture that Mary began to scream uncontrollably. She was no longer herself. She was rolling on the floor and was soon screaming at the top of her voice.

Together with a team of lay persons, I began to minister to her, believing that the Lord would release her and set her free from the bondage of the demonic spirits. As we called on the name of the Lord, Mary continued to scream. She placed both her hands on her throat as though wanting to strangle herself and screamed until her voice became sore. When she regained control of herself, she told the team to refrain from calling the name of the Lord because she would be screaming again against her wishes.

As we continued to pray for her, Mary remained in her state of derangement. In the midst of one of these episodes I decided to talk to Mary. Although Mary appeared as though she was in a state of demon possession, I knew from the way she responded that she was well aware of what was happening to her and around her. Speaking into her ears, I said to her, 'Mary, if you can hear me, say, "Jesus is Lord".' I wanted her to affirm the Lordship of Christ.

Mary struggled to affirm the Lordship of Christ. But just when she was about to say 'Jesus is Lord', a demonic spirit would take over her vocal cords and say 'Jesus is not Lord'. The team continued to pray and encouraged her to affirm the fact that 'Jesus is Lord'. After much struggle, and after two hours of ministry, Mary could at last declare the Lordship of Christ. The moment she affirmed Jesus as Lord, her screaming ceased and she was released from the power and grip of the demonic spirits.

I felt led to counsel further with Mary. As I spoke to her, I realized that Mary had harboured hurt feelings. She had suffered from an inferiority complex and for some time had harboured hatred and bitterness against her colleagues who had bullied her. She also harboured bitterness against her family whom she felt had looked down on her because of her inability to earn more than her other siblings. To make matters worse, she had for some time been having an affair with a married man and the sense of guilt was overwhelming her.

I spoke to her of the love of God and the fact that God loved her as she was. That afternoon, Mary cried her heart out. She poured out all her grievances; she expressed her hatred for her colleagues and the resentment she had for her family. Through the process of counselling, Mary repented of her sins, sought forgiveness for her bitterness and hatred, and was released from the bondage of the evil one. I also met with Mary's parents, and after several sessions of counselling with Mary and her parents, she finally found herself able to cope with the stress of life. Mary became a Christian, and so did her family. Mary had become free because Jesus had set her free.

As Christian counsellors, we need to be ready for cases of all types. Although not all Christian counsellors would want to be engaged in a ministry of deliverance and release as related above, it is imperative for the Christian counsellor to understand symptoms associated with demonization so that the necessary referrals can be made.

When a person is demonized, he lives in fear. Not only is he affected, but his whole family is as well. It is in these situations that the comfort of Jesus can be experienced through the ministry of deliverance and release.

The biblical commission to be engaged in this ministry of deliverance and release is quite clear. Jesus in Mark 16:15–18 says,

> '*Go into all the world and preach the gospel to all creation. He who has believed and has been baptized*

> *shall be saved: but he who has disbelieved shall be condemned. And these signs will accompany those who have believed: in My name they will cast out demons, they will speak with new tongues; they will pick up serpents, and if they drink any deadly poison, it shall not hurt them; they will lay hands on the sick, and they will recover.'*

Jesus says in the above text that in His name His followers will cast out demons. If demonization is discerned and the process of counselling demands the expulsion of demons residing in the counsellee, then the Christian counsellor can exercise the authority given to Him by Jesus to expel the demon and release the counsellee from demonic bondage.

Demon possession is not something new. The Bible, in several passages, records incidents of such a nature. The Greek word that is used to describe the phenomenon is *daimonizomai* (Matthew 4:24; Mark 1:32; 5:15–16). This word means 'to be possessed by a demon' or 'to act under the control of a demon'. A person who is demon possessed is in fact under the control of a demonic spirit or spirits. He is not able to control himself and acts under the control of the demon.

Biblical Case Studies

The Bible records a number of incidents where Jesus or the name of Jesus has brought about deliverance and release for those in a state of demon possession. A classic illustration is that of the Gerasene Demoniac that is recorded in Mark 5:1–20.

The Gerasene Demoniac

In this story, we are told that, while at the country of the Gerasenes, Jesus was met by a man who was possessed with an unclean spirit. Under the control of the demonic spirit he had acquired enormous strength. This prevented anyone from binding him with chains. There were none who could subdue him. And so day and night, among the tombs and in the mountains, he would cry and gash himself with stones.

When the demoniac encountered Jesus, he cried with a loud voice saying, '*What do I have to do with You, Jesus, Son of the Most High God? I implore You by God, do not torment me!*' This cry was in response to Jesus' command to the demonic spirit to come out of the man (verse 8).

A dialogue between the demons and Jesus soon ensued with the final expulsion of the demons from the man into a herd of about two thousand pigs which drowned after rushing down a steep bank and into the sea. The end result was the deliverance and release of the demoniac from the control of demons. His mind was restored, and he was asked to tell his people the great things that the Lord had done for him.

The Slave Girl at Philippi

The second biblical incident that we would like to relate before we make some observations, is found in Acts 16:16–18. In this incident, Paul is approached by a slave girl who is possessed by a spirit of divination. She was bringing her masters much profit by fortune-telling. On meeting Paul and his company, she cried out, '*These men are bond-servants of the Most High God, who are proclaiming to you the way of salvation.*' This she did for many days. Paul greatly annoyed said to the spirit, '*I command you in the name of Jesus Christ to come out of her!*' And it came out at that very moment.

Some Observations

It would be proper at this juncture to make some observations regarding demons and demonization in the light of these two passages.

Firstly, the passages affirm the existence of demonic

spirits. These demonic spirits are subordinate to Satan who is their ruler (Matthew 12:24–29). Although the Bible does not say very much about the origin of Satan, his existence nonetheless is taken for granted in Scripture (see Isaiah 14:12–15).

Secondly, demons are possessed with certain powers. They can reside in man and animals (Mark 5:2, 13; Acts 16:16); they can control the faculties of man and through them exhibit preternatural knowledge (Mark 5:7; Acts 16:16–17), and preternatural strength (Mark 5:3–4).

Thirdly, demons torment the demonized. The demonized are compelled to do things that are beyond their wishes (Mark 5:5). They are made to look dreadful and pitiful in the sight of man. Sometimes the demonized are afflicted with sickness like epilepsy (Mark 9:14–29), dumbness (Matthew 9:32), and even blindness (Matthew 12:22).

Fourthly, demons feel uncomfortable in the presence of Jesus (Mark 5:7) or in the presence of those who exalt Jesus as Lord (Acts 16:17).

Fifthly, the passages affirm the fact that demons can be expelled from the demonized in the name of Jesus.

Drawing from the above, it seems to us that there are three major steps in the ministry of deliverance and release. The first is the **encounter**. Here, the counsellor ascertains whether the counsellee is demonized or not. This includes a time of probing and listening. Should there be obvious symptoms of a condition that can be handled by a medical practitioner or a psychiatrist, then the necessary referrals should be made. The second step is the **expulsion**. Here the demonic spirit is commanded to leave the demon-possessed by the authority and name of Jesus. This is seen in both the biblical cases mentioned above. The third step is the **follow-up**. Although, we are not told what Paul did to the slave girl following the deliverance, we can assume that she was absorbed into the caring community of the early Church for further ministry. In the case of the Gerasene Demoniac, the counsel of Jesus was evident. Jesus told him to go and report to his people the great things that the Lord had done for him.

THE THREE MAJOR STEPS IN THE PROCESS OF DELIVERANCE AND RELEASE

The Encounter

A Spiritual Warfare

A Christian counsellor must recognise that when he is engaged in the ministry of deliverance and release, he is in fact engaged in spiritual warfare. The Christian battles not with enemies that can be seen, but with spiritual enemies that are unseen. As the Apostle Paul puts it, we battle *'not against flesh and blood, but against the rulers, against the powers, against the world forces of this darkness, against the spiritual forces of wickedness in the heavenly places'* (Ephesians 6:12).

Some Christians may be cynical about the presence of demonic spirits and their activity in the lives of people. When a person behaves abnormally, they send him to a mental institution or to a psychiatrist. They would not even consider the possibility of demonization. Yet the Bible is quite clear about the work of demonic spirits in the lives of people. Paul says that we 'struggle' or 'wrestle' against spiritual forces of wickedness in the heavenly places. In the ministry of deliverance and release, we are in fact wrestling with the powers of darkness at close quarters. The good news of the Gospel however is the fact that in Christ we have the victory over Satan and his cohorts.

We cannot fully understand how demons enter the body of humans. It is possible that the demons gain entry when a person indulges in activities that are conducive to demonic interference. If he indulges in evil thoughts, evil deeds and evil actions, he is in fact providing the demonic spirits a foothold in his life. In this way, demons find a lodging place in a person and seek to destroy and control him.

A case in point is the life of King Saul. You will remember that Saul was God's anointed king when the Jewish people asked God for a king (1 Samuel 10). Not only was he chosen as king, the Spirit of God was also upon him. But when King Saul became proud and began to disobey God, we are told in Scripture that *'the Spirit of the Lord departed from Saul and an evil spirit from the Lord terrorized him'* (1 Samuel 16:14). In other words, God allowed an evil spirit to torment him. His sin became the entry point for the evil spirit to do its work. That could have accounted for his weird behaviour and the attempts made on the life of David (1 Samuel 18:10, 11; 19:9–10; 28:15).

Some time ago, I (Isaac) ministered to a young man who was demonized. Through the process of counselling and ministry, I discovered that the man was in fact a homosexual who had been steeped in homosexual activities for many years. This young man attempted to free himself from activities that he felt were destroying him physically. In his case, he felt that his homosexuality was the result of demonic influence in his life. He recognised that the only way to deliverance and freedom from the bondage of demonic powers, was Christ. He received Christ as Lord and Saviour, and that same day experienced deliverance from demonic bondage. Jesus had released him from the clutches of the evil one to experience freedom in Him.

Demon possession is a fact that cannot be denied. People do get possessed, and we who believe that Jesus is the answer are called to bring hope and deliverance into the lives of these people, so that they can be released and set free through the power and name of Jesus.

A lady was once brought to me (Shirley) because she would often be gripped by an uncontrollable tremor when she joined a prayer group. The tremor resembled the shaking and vibrating movements of 'mediums' in the Chinese temple in a trance. The counselling encounter revealed that her brother with whom she lived was a medium or one who had access to the spirit world. Her close identification with her brother and her fear of losing his love kept her from telling her brother about her commitment to Christ. Consequently, she had been living with a sense of guilt and fear for some years. She was one day made to take part in a ritual her brother performed at home and she succumbed in fear. She felt a gripping sensation across her chest and the next day sought help from Christians, who brought her to me. The series of counselling sessions that followed included prayers for deliverance. The deliverance from the seizures was complete when she decided to make a stand for the Lord and not only tell her brother about her love for Christ but also pray for his salvation as well.

Demonic spirits may gain entry into our lives when we persist in sin; when we allow hatred, resentment, anger, unforgiveness, sexual perversions, lust, pornography and the like to overwhelm us. When we allow these negative traits to persist in our being, we are in fact opening ourselves to the dominance of Satan and his demonic cohorts who may find a lodging place in our lives.

Some have asked if Christians can be demon possessed. If we are talking about Spirit-filled Christians who walk close to the Lord and are growing in Him, it is not possible for them to be demon possessed. But Christians can be demonized and even possessed if they live carnal lives or if a residual part of their pagan past is still left unrenounced. In some instances, some past experiences have caused inner damage in the lives of Christians and these have been suppressed and allowed to fester, providing a foothold for the evil one.

We have observed that sometimes a new convert may manifest a demonic presence in his life. This is not because demonic spirits have just entered the young Christian's life, but that the demonic spirits within him are now wanting to get out. These, having found a lodging place in his life due to his pagan past, may now be finding it uncomfortable dwelling in the life of this new convert, and are attempting either to cause the new convert to return to his pagan ways or to come out of him. We have found that a ministry of deliverance will enable this new convert to experience total release.

How do we prepare ourselves for these encounters?

The Counsellor's Preparation

Before an encounter takes place, it is important for the counsellor or counsellors engaged in the ministry to be convinced that demonization is a reality and that persons can receive deliverance and wholeness in the name of Jesus. It is foolhardy to enter a warfare of this nature without being spiritually prepared. Because the Christian counsellor is engaged in spiritual warfare, he needs to be in a right relationship with God. He needs to be holy unto the Lord. Not to take cognizance of the importance of a right relationship with God is to enter spiritual warfare unprepared.

You will remember the story in Acts 19:14–19, how the seven sons of Sceva (who was a Jewish priest) attempted to cast out an evil spirit in the name of Jesus but without success. The response of the evil spirits to their command was this *'I recognize Jesus, and I know about Paul, but who are you?'* And the Bible says that *'the man, in whom was the evil spirit, leaped on them and subdued all of them and overpowered them, so that they fled out of that house naked and wounded.'*

The problem with the sons of Sceva was that they themselves did not know the risen Lord in a personal way. They attempted to ape what Paul was doing in the ministry of deliverance. They did not know Jesus, and were spiritually unprepared for the task. They used the name of Jesus as a kind of magical formula hoping to see the expulsion of the demonic spirit. Their experience was tragic as they left the scene naked and wounded.

The counsellor engaged in a ministry of deliverance must recognize that it is Jesus dwelling within him that the demonic spirits are afraid of. He comes not in his own authority, but the authority of Jesus. It is in the Name and Authority of Jesus that the demons are cast out.

The counsellor engaged in a ministry of deliverance must recognise that he is entering spiritual warfare. He needs to come clothed in the armour of God. The Apostle Paul in Ephesians 6:10–17 says:

10 *Finally, be strong in the Lord, and in the strength of His might.*

11 *Put on the full armour of God, that you may be able to stand firm against the schemes of the devil.*

12 *For our struggle is not against flesh and blood, but against the rulers, against the powers, against the world forces of this darkness, against spiritual forces of wickedness in the heavenly places.*

13 *Therefore, take up the full armour of God, that you may be able to resist in the evil day, and having done everything, to stand firm.*

14 *Stand firm therefore, **having girded your loins with truth and having put on the breastplate of righteousness,***

15 *and having shod **your feet with the preparation of the gospel of peace;***

16 *in addition to all, taking up the shield of faith with which you will be able to extinguish all the flaming missiles of the evil one.*

17 *And take **the helmet of salvation**, and the sword of the Spirit, which is the word of God.*

The exhortation of Paul for us is to be strong in the Lord

and in the strength of His might. We cannot enter spiritual warfare with a negative spirit; we need to enter spiritual warfare with the faith that victory is already ours.

Since our enemies are the unseen *'spiritual forces of wickedness in the heavenly places'*, we come also prepared by putting on spiritually, not part of the armour of God, but as the Apostle Paul puts it, *'the full armour of God'*. The goal in wearing the armour of God is to resist the devil and to stand firm.

What sort of armour was Paul talking about? He was speaking of an armour that consisted of the following:

1. *The Belt of Truth* (Ephesians 6:14)

In the Roman armour, the belt was tied tightly around the waist to indicate that the soldier was prepared for battle. It was used to tuck up his tunic, and to hold his weapons in position.

The Christian is called to wear the belt of truth all the time. The belt of truth reflects the very texture of the Christian's character. If he lives in truth, then he in fact lives in freedom because the 'truth will set him free'. When a Christian lives in 'truth', he lives in the will of God. He knows his rights as a child of God, and stands ready for spiritual warfare. The Christian wearing the belt of truth gives no opportunity for the devil to create confusion. He is able thus to offer the Word of Truth as guiding principles to the counsellee.

2. *The Breastplate of Righteousness* (Ephesians 6:14)

The breastplate covered the soldier from the neck to the thighs both in the front and back. It was to protect the heart of the soldier. The Christian wearing the breastplate of righteousness, enters spiritual warfare with a clear conscience. His character before God and man is blameless, and he stands for uprightness and integrity. In putting this piece of armour on, he prevents the devil from pointing an accusing finger at him.

3. *Feet shod with the preparation of the Gospel of Peace* (Ephesians 6:15)

Roman soldiers wore strong army footwear to enable them to embark on long marches. The Christian, like a soldier, is always ready to share the gospel of peace wherever he goes. He not only shares the gospel of peace, but he also experiences the gospel of peace. In declaring the gospel message, he is in fact engaged in spiritual warfare as he tears down the strongholds of the evil one with the message of peace. The counsellor moves in the offensive against the evil one in the ministry of deliverance. He is not in a defensive or passive position.

4. *The shield of faith* (Ephesians 6:16)

The Roman shield is large and oval in shape and is held in front of a Roman soldier for protection. It is four and a half feet in length and two and a half feet wide and consisted of two layers of wood glued together and covered with linen and hide and bound with iron.

For the Christian, his protective shield is faith. It is faith in the Word of God, and faith in the God who keeps His Word. It is believing that God can do what He has said and promised in His Word. This faith in a great God serves as the Christian's shield and wards off the flaming missiles of the devil.

When Paul talked about the flaming missiles, he was referring to the arrows that were dipped in pitch, ignited, and fired at the enemy. Sometimes, before engaging in battle, soldiers would dip their shields in water as a method of extinguishing the flaming missiles.

When we engage in spiritual warfare, Satan attacks us with his flaming missiles. He attacks us and our family intending to cripple us and weaken our witness. But we praise God that this is not possible when we ward the attacks with the shield of faith. As we exercise faith in God and enter a battle with His authority, we are victorious.

5. *The Helmet of Salvation* (Ephesians 6:17)

The Roman helmet was made of bronze. Like any helmet it protected the head. The head, being the nerve centre and very vulnerable is preserved by the helmet. The Christian's spiritual helmet is salvation. The Christian is preserved from eternal death because he has salvation in Christ Jesus. This sets his mind free from the fear of death and makes him eternally secure because, whether in this life or in the next, he is with God. His soul is protected eternally from the evil one and so he enters spiritual battle without any fear.

6. *The Sword of the Spirit* (Ephesians 6:17)

The sword is a soldier's weapon of offence as well as defence. It is a short two-edged cut-and-thrust sword which the soldier uses to kill, or to protect himself.

The Christian's sword is the word of God. The 'word of God' in this context has to do with divine utterance or speech. Whilst this 'word' could be the word of wisdom or the word of knowledge and discernment that the Spirit gives in the midst of spiritual warfare, it is also the word of Scripture that the Lord brings to our remembrance that can be used to defeat Satan. Was this not the way Jesus overcame the Tempter (Matthew 4)? It is as the Christian wears the full armour of God that he is ready to enter a warfare against demonic spirits and receive the Lord's victory.

Interviewing the Counsellee

When a demonized counsellee is brought to a counsellor, he is normally coherent unless he is brought to you already in a possessed state. Although he may be coherent, he is in fact demonized. We use the word 'demonized' to refer to one who has a demonic spirit or spirits within him. There are many levels of demonization. It may vary from mild to severe. Demonization is considered mild when a person is said to be under demonic subjection or oppression. Demonization is considered severe when a person is said to be under demonic possession.

A person who is under demonic subjection discovers that he is unable to respond to the gospel (2 Corinthians 4:4); he finds himself bound and obsessed by sinful activity (2 Peter 2:1–12) and incapable of resisting evil tendencies. A person who is under demonic oppression finds himself intermittently disturbed by nightmares, extreme fears or uncontrollable moods (e.g. King Saul).

A person who is under demonic attack often finds himself losing control over himself. The demons might torment him and make him do things against his will. In many of these cases, demonic spirits actually reside in the demonized. When the demonic spirits take control of a person, he is said to be possessed. In some cases when the demonized is in a state of possession, he is aware of what is happening around him although he may not be in control of himself. On the other hand, he may enter a state of trance and become oblivious to his environment and will not remember the episode on gaining consciousness.

Whilst it is easier to handle mild cases of demonization, it takes more experience to handle the more severe cases of demonization. The points that follow are attempts to assist the lay counsellor in dealing with some of these cases.

When a counsellee is brought to the counsellor, it is important for the counsellor to diagnose the case and to ascertain if it is a case of demonization or psychosis. If it is a case of psychosis or mental disorder, the counsellor should refer the counsellee to a psychiatrist. If the counsellor is uncertain as to whether the counsellee is in fact possessed, he should refer the counsellee to a more experienced counsellor for assistance. Christian counsellors should not declare a counsellee possessed if they are not certain if it is so. To do so is to plant unnecessary fear in the counsellee who is already emotionally disturbed.

A preliminary interview with the counsellee and close family members or friends is necessary before we move into the **expulsion** phase. This will enable the counsellor to gather valuable information about the counsellee which will assist him in his ministry. It would be helpful to know a little of the background of the counsellee, his family, and events that led him to his present state. It is also important to find out if the counsellee has been involved in occult practices as there is often a correlation between occultic practices and demon possession. We may ask if the counsellee has:

1. Dabbled in black magic, witchcraft, temple rites, Satan worship.
2. Consulted spirit mediums, clairvoyants, fortune tellers, palm readers, and other religious practitioners.
3. Taken part in séances and ouija board activities.
4. Sought healing through pagan religious practitioners, through psychic healing and psychic surgery with the resultant use of charms, holy water, amulets, talismans, pagan religious objects, etc.

During the process of counselling, the counsellor would be able to ascertain whether a counsellee is demonized by noting the following:

1. Has the counsellee been oppressed by any evil or destructive emotions that are contrary to his own will or nature? (For example, hatred, an uncontrollable bitterness, resentment, fear, jealousy, impatience, pride, etc.)
2. Has the counsellee appeared restless, talkative, unreasonable, showing extreme fluctuation of moods?
3. Is the counsellee going through deep depression? Is he resorting to self-pity?
4. Is he enslaved to sexual immorality, homosexuality, lesbianism, unclean thoughts? Is he enslaved to alcohol, or drugs, etc?

5.   Does he resort to blasphemy, mockery, and unclean language?

When indications point to demonization, the counsellor can then proceed with the ministry of deliverance.

The Expulsion

The expulsion process begins with the demonized desiring to be delivered. It is important that the counsellor asks the counsellee if he desires to be released from demonic bondage. The counsellor should share the gospel with the counsellee and explain to him that deliverance is only possible through Christ and that it is imperative that he accepts Christ if deliverance is to be complete. The counsellor should be slow in moving into a ministry of deliverance if the counsellee is unwilling to accept Christ as Saviour and Lord. To do so is to clean a house of demons only to invite more to come in (Luke 11:24–26).

If members of a family bring the counsellee for deliverance, then they should also be told the seriousness of the counsellee's condition and the part they can play in getting him well. The family of the counsellee could also be counselled and challenged to consider the Christian gospel for themselves. They too should turn to the Lord in repentance if they are to assist their loved one to recovery. In our experience, a number of families have been won to Christ through this means.

If the counsellee desires to be released from demonic bondage, ask the following questions:

1.   Will you accept Jesus Christ as your Saviour, Master and Deliverer? (If the counsellee does not know the gospel, then it is imperative that the counsellor explains the content of the gospel message.)
2.   Will you renounce Satan and all his works of darkness in your life?
3.   Will you renounce all involvement with occult activity?

4.   Will you forgive the person against whom you have held bitterness and resentment?
5.   Will you forgive yourself?
6.   Will you forsake questionable activities?

The counsellor should take time to talk to the counsellee about the above issues and to ascertain the extent to which the counsellee is involved in some of these activities. Having asked these questions, the counsellee should be led to pray to receive Christ as Lord. If for some reason the counsellee is not ready to pray with the counsellor, ministry should go on until such time as the counsellee is ready to pray to receive Christ.

When a person is demonized, we believe that demons can be expelled through prayer. However, every counsellor engaged in the ministry of deliverance, should recognize the following:

1.   He must recognise that God has given him the authority over demonic spirits, and they can be cast out in the name of Jesus (Mark 16:15ff).
2.   He must recognise that there is power in the name and blood of Jesus (Philippians 2:9–11; Ephesians 1:7; 1 John 1:7; Romans 5:9; Revelation 12:11).
3.   He must come with the empowerment of the Holy Spirit and the recognition that the gifts of the Spirit are available for him in His ministry (Acts 1:8; 1 Corinthians 12:4–11).
4.   He must come to 'battle' clothed in the armour of God as related in Ephesians 6:11–17.
5.   He must face the battle with a clean heart (Psalm 66:18).
6.   He must come with the recognition that it is God who is going to win the battle and not the counsellor himself.

Deliverance comes through prayer. When praying for deliverance, the counsellor should pray with confidence and faith. The counsellor should come against the demonic spirit or spirits, and bind them in the name of

Jesus. Sometimes, during prayer, the demonized begins to manifest symptoms of demon possession. This is indicated by some of the following symptoms:

1. His eyes are glazed or unnaturally bright and protruding or unable to focus naturally.

2. Sometimes he froths in the mouth or exudes fetid breath.

3. There is a change in personality. He somehow manifests a change in intelligence, or moral character, or demeanour, or appearance.

4. There is sometimes also a change in his physical makeup. Sometimes he demonstrates the possession of unusual strength. We once ministered to a young boy who was demon possessed. Although he was young, he had the ability to perform feats that were startling. Untrained, he had the strength to bend iron rods and to perform martial arts. But whilst some are possessed with unusual strength, others manifest a loss of strength and appear anaemic; sometimes they become epileptic and foam in the mouth; sometimes they are numbed to pain; sometimes there is also a change of voice.

5. There is sometimes a change in mental ability. The demonized may seem to possess occult and psychic powers like telepathy, clairvoyance and the ability to predict. Sometimes they possess unusual knowledge of things, and even understand languages unknown to them. We were once ministering to an elderly lady who when in a state of demon possession could predict by name the people who were to enter into the room. She could for example accurately predict: 'Pastor Isaac Lim is coming up the stairs now.' In a few minutes, Isaac walked in as she had predicted. The reality of the powers of darkness is not to be denied. It is sad to see good and sweet-natured persons gripped by a strange power. We certainly, in compassion, exercise the authority Christ gives to His children to release the captives in His name.

6. There is often a definite aversion to Christ and reaction to the name of Jesus. A counsellee once shouted out 'Don't mention the name of Jesus!'

When the counsellor ministers deliverance, he addresses the demonic spirit and says, 'I command you in the name of Jesus to come out of him/her.' This command is in fact used by Paul in Philippi. We need to note a few things about this command.

Firstly, it is an address of authority. It is not an appeal to the demonic spirit to leave, but it is a command to leave. There should be no hesitation when a command of this nature is made. The counsellor can speak quietly, but he needs to address the demonic spirit with authority.

Secondly, the counsellor addresses the demonic spirit, not in his own authority, but in the name of Jesus Christ. It is in the name of Jesus that the demons must bow in the acknowledgement of His Lordship over all of creation. Paul says in Philippians 2:10–11 *'That at the name of Jesus every knee should bow, of those who are in heaven and on earth, and under the earth, and that every tongue should confess that Jesus Christ is Lord to the glory of God the Father.'* The disciples of Jesus understood the power of His name when they said, *'Lord, even the demons are subject to us in Your name'* (Luke 10:17).

Thirdly, the counsellor, if he knows the name of the demonic spirit, should address the demonic spirit by its name (Mark 5:9). It should be noted as well that there are times when the demonic spirit does not want to reveal its identity. At other times it gives fake names to confuse the counsellor. In these situations, the counsellor can still expel the demonic spirit in the name of Jesus and not be side-tracked into 'name-hunting'.

Fourthly, the counsellor should command the demonic spirit to come out or depart. The counsellor does not appeal or plead for the demonic spirit to depart. He commands the demonic spirit to depart. Sometimes the demonic spirit might respond by refusing to depart. I

(Isaac) remember ministering to a lady possessed by several demons. As I commanded the demons to depart, a voice responded by saying, 'I do not want to go. I like to remain here.' To this question I replied by saying, 'If you do not leave this child of God now, then I will ask Jesus to torment you.' Immediately there was a loud scream, and the demons left the lady and she was delivered. The name of Jesus has power and authority.

There are certain signs to indicate the departure of demonic spirits. Normally a person who is demonized will know whether a spirit has left him or not. Some time ago, we prayed for a woman who had come to the altar for ministry. She requested prayers for a troubled marriage relationship. As we prayed for her, she began to sway and then to manifest signs of being demonized. She told us that the demon was in her stomach and then as we continued to pray, she told us that it had moved to her head. She held her head as though in pain. We laboured in prayer, and suddenly she went limp. We asked her if the demonic spirit was still there. With a smile of relief on her face, she said that it had left her.

Demonic spirits leave a person in many ways. Sometimes it leaves a person quietly. Sometimes it leaves with a loud scream. At other times several screams can be heard as various spirits leave the body. Sometimes, the counsellee vomits out thick phlegm as the spirit leaves. At other times the counsellee just testifies to a deliverance although nothing spectacular has happened.

There is no one way to deliverance or one formula to deliverance. We should not allow ourselves to be trapped into believing that demons can leave a person in only one particular way.

There are times when the demonic spirits attempt to deceive the counsellor by telling the counsellor through the voice of the demonized that everything is well and that he is all right. The counsellor should not be fooled because Satan is in fact the father of lies.

We once ministered to a lady who was severely demonized. As we ministered to her, she seemed to be responding well, and after an hour of ministry, she turned to us and said, 'I am now all right. You can go home. You are very tired, you need to go home and rest.' At that moment, the Lord revealed to us that it was not the counsellee who was speaking, but the demon in her. This led us to another round of prayers for deliverance.

As Christian counsellors, we need to be cautious about demonic deception. When deliverance takes place, the counsellor and his team will know it because the Holy Spirit will reveal it to them. Moreover, the counsellee will also tell the counsellor that he is well. However, if deliverance is not forthcoming after several hours of ministry, it is best to call the ministry to a halt and resume it another day. This is to conserve physical energy and at the same time allow the team time for spiritual refreshment in preparation for the next encounter.

It is normally advisable to engage in the ministry of deliverance as a team. A few lay counsellors under the leadership of a counselling Elder should minister together as a deliverance team under the supervision of a pastor or elder. Team members should be in an attitude of prayer with one member of the team taking the lead each time. The team should be of one mind, consulting each other during the process of ministry.

Once deliverance takes place, the follow-up begins.

The Follow-up:
Effecting the Christian Experience

Although the ministry of deliverance may be over, the work of counselling continues. If the counsellee is a new Christian, the counsellor needs to teach him how to pray and to resist the devil. As the devil will attempt to lead this new convert back to his old ways, resisting the devil is very important. As James puts it, *'Submit therefore to God. Resist the devil and he will flee from you'* (James 4:7). A similar exhortation is made by the apostle Peter. He says:

> *'Be of sober spirit, be on the alert. Your adversary, the devil, prowls about like a roaring lion, seeking someone to devour. But resist him, firm in your faith, knowing that the same experiences of suffering are being accomplished by your brethren who are in the world. And after you have suffered for a little while, the God of all grace, who called you to His eternal glory in Christ, will Himself perfect, confirm, strengthen and establish you.'*   (1 Peter 5:8–10)

One of the ways to resist the devil is for the counsellee to take authority in the name of Jesus and command the demonic spirits to leave him alone and not to disturb him anymore. Whenever evil or negative thoughts disturb the counsellee, he should command these thoughts to be gone in the name of Jesus.

It would be wise, if the counsellee is a new Christian, to introduce him to the Caring Group or a small Group. Getting him attached to a small Group is a means through which he can receive ministry. New Christians need spiritual support from a community, and this can best be obtained in a small Group setting.

If the counsellee has emotional problems, then proper counselling is necessary. If during the encounter he has shared hurts, and has asked the Lord to help him in his desire to forgive those who have hurt him, then the counsellor should continue to help him to work that out in order that inner healing can be experienced.

We have seen the power of God's love, as expressed through the Body of Christ, transforming persons. There is an underlying human need that can only be fulfilled by the love of Christ. The Christian community can reflect this love by providing a supportive fellowship in ways the counsellee can understand. Hence counsellors cannot work alone.

A counsellee shared with me (Shirley) her reflections on her encounters with the powers of darkness. She said, 'Mrs Lim, I don't know what I would have done if not for the love and support of all of you. I was terrified of this "thing" that tormented me. At times I was afraid that even my husband would think that I was insane and making these things up. The worst fear I had was that no one would believe that I actually "heard voices". If not for the love of my Christian friends, I would most probably have taken my own life. Now I only want to be that kind of a Christian friend to help others even if I cannot be a good counsellor. Please call on me if there is anything I can do.'

Perhaps this counsellee's observations sum up the horror and isolation of the demonized and the role the Body of Christ can play in offering a ministry of deliverance and release. Will you also commit your services as part of this Caring Community?

Chapter 8

A Ministry of Prayer

One of the most important components in the ministry of Christian counselling is the practice of prayer. Something happens when prayer is offered to God on behalf of the counsellee. There is something wonderful that occurs when the counsellor seeks the face of God in earnest and intercedes for the counsellee.

In one of our sessions on the 'Basics of Christian Counselling', a young girl came up for ministry. She grew up in a broken home and found herself handicapped by a deep sense of insecurity. I (Isaac) took time to counsel and pray with her. During the time of prayer, the Holy Spirit ministered to this young lady who later wrote this testimony which I am publishing with her concurrence:

'I can never forget the night of May 26, 1987 and it is my constant prayer that I will always remember that night. I want to share what the Lord has done for me because I'm truly grateful to Him for coming down to my level and meeting my needs.

My faith in the Lord is rather weak and I need to feel or see something before I can really believe. But God has touched my life in order that I may feel His presence and believe in Him.

I come from a broken family and as such have suffered emotional hurts as a result of my past.

143

Because of my emotional problems, I have been crippled in my relationship with God and people. Although I came to know Christ in my school days, I never experienced the new life which the Bible talks about. Joy, peace and love are terms I've experienced only recently. The pains and hurts of my childhood and teenage years are responsible for my present emotional state. I have found it difficult to receive love because I've never been loved by my mum or dad. Consequently, I have found it difficult to accept God's love and forgiveness.

My background has also made me a very insecure person. I have never been cared for and have had to learn how to fend for myself. As a result, I have learned not to trust anyone.

I hold a low image of myself. I consider myself of little worth. Perhaps, this is due to the fact that I have been constantly rejected by my mother. I have no confidence in myself and often think I deserve the worst in life. I do not see any good in me.

I have had a lot of fears and the one that has tormented me has been the fear of demon possession. I also feel nervous communicating with people because I'm afraid they will know the true 'me' and would not like what they know. So you see, I've lots of weaknesses and need God's healing touch. I'm also afraid to share my problems with any pastor or counsellor because of what they might say if they knew me.

I believe the Lord led me to Wesley Church for this course on the Basics of Christian Counselling. My friend signed up for the course and persuaded me to join him. I agreed to go along because I wanted to find out how I could help myself. On one occasion, when Rev. Lim was talking about demon possession I became fearful because that was one of my fears. I went home that night afraid and troubled. I was afraid of attending the next session but somehow, by God's grace I found my way there.

I was actually shivering with fear when I approached Rev. Lim after the session. I was very apprehensive about our encounter. I began by asking him a few questions just to feel at ease. Finally I shared with him my problems. Rev. Lim prayed for me as he identified the inner hurts that I had been harbouring for many years. He prayed for the healing of my memories; memories of the past which had affected me and caused me to be what I am today.

During the prayer, when he mentioned an incident in the past which had affected me or hurt me, I would shiver and cry. But strangely, for a moment, my mind went blank, not focusing on anything. I believe I must have been crying out those pains and hurts of the past. I began to experience a tremendous warmth and peace resting on me. It was a peace that surpassed all understanding filling each part of me. I felt loved; I felt comforted. Every part of me felt comforted and loved. It was as if God was comforting me after removing each thorn that had hurt me. After praying, I felt so light, refreshed and peaceful.

I thank God for what he has done for me. I want to share about my life because I want to give God the glory that belongs to Him. The Lord is indeed my Saviour for He has delivered and redeemed me from my miseries. He has filled my heart with His love and peace. He has put within me a gentle and quiet spirit. Praise the Lord.

Christian counselling is not complete without the ministry of prayer. When we pray, we are affirming the fact that God is the ultimate source of all wholeness and healing. It is as we bring the needs of the counsellee before God's throne of grace that He ministers and meets the counsellee at his point of need.

If prayer is to play a significant part in Christian counselling, then the counsellor must be a person of prayer. He prays before he counsels, he prays while he counsels, and he prays after he has counselled. He is in constant communion with God for direction, discernment, and wisdom as he counsels.

Whilst the counsellor ministers to both Christians as well as non-Christians, he is under no obligation to play down the place of prayer in his counselling process. The counsellee who approaches a Christian counsellor for ministry is normally aware that he will be counselled within a particular religious framework and that prayer is a part of the counselling process.

In our experience, we have always found our counsellees responding readily to prayer. In almost all our cases when we have asked if they would like for us to pray for them or with them, their answers have been in the affirmative. There is power in prayer. We must remember that.

Prayer and the Christian Counsellor

The Christian counsellor enters the counselling process in the spirit of prayer. He recognizes his inadequacies and his need for the Spirit's guidance and direction. As he counsels, the Lord directs him, and he is able to be a source of help to the counsellee. Christian counsellors need constantly to be in harmony with God. It is in Him that we are able to minister His love and peace to all in need.

The Bible affirms the importance of prayer in the lives of God's servants. Those who have been greatly used by God have been people of prayer. We think of Abraham, Moses, David, Elijah, Daniel and a host of others. All these were effective servants because they were persons of prayer.

Jesus, the counsellor par excellence, was Himself a Man

of Prayer. The Bible tells us that He would spend the early hours of the morning in prayer (Mark 1:35). He would also take time out in the midst of a very hectic ministry to pray (Luke 4:42; 5:16; Matthew 14:23). What did He pray about? Most probably, He would, among other things, have brought the needs of those whom He ministered to before God's throne of grace.

If Jesus needed to spend time in prayer, what about us? Our prayer life essentially determines our effectiveness in the counselling ministry.

What Happens When Prayer is Offered

God does something when the counsellor prays for the counsellee. But what actually happens? To help us answer this question, we are going to use James 5:13–16 as our reference point. James says,

> 13 *Is anyone among you suffering? Let him pray. Is anyone cheerful? Let him sing praises.*
> 14 *Is anyone among you sick? Let him call for the elders of the church, and let them pray over him, anointing him with oil in the name of the Lord;*
> 15 *and the prayer offered in faith will restore the one who is sick, and the Lord will raise him up, and if he has committed sins, they will be forgiven him.*
> 16 *Therefore, confess your sins to one another, and pray for one another so that you may be healed. The effective prayer of a righteous man can accomplish much.*

A cursory look at this text would point to the fact that the context has to do with prayers offered for the physically sick. A closer look at the text would however reveal a larger application. Prayer here need not be limited to the physically sick, but can refer also to those who are going through emotional distress.

According to W.E. Oesterley the word 'suffering' in

verse 13 includes 'mental worry or distress'.[1] From this we can see the importance of prayer in the ministry of inner healing.

There are three very important words in James 5:15 that assist us in understanding the power of prayer in the context of counselling. The first is the word 'restore'. The second is the word 'raise'. The third is the word 'forgiven'.

1. Prayer Restores

The word 'restore' (in the NASV) comes from the Greek word which can also be translated to mean 'to save', 'to heal', or 'to make whole'. Prayer as such restores the emotional equilibrium of the counsellee. It saves him from further affliction. It aids the process of healing and wholeness. There is a positive forward thrust in prayer. The counsellee receives deliverance from his infirmities or sufferings.

Through our prayers, God restores (Psalm 23:3) the troubled and weary. We have seen counsellees coming to us in anger only to experience a release through the ministry of prayer. We have seen counsellees under deep spiritual bondage being set free through prayer, into a new relationship with Jesus. Prayer has healed memories, mended damaged emotions, removed resentments, melted bitterness and anger, and has caused the grace of God to flow as a healing stream, bringing relief and cleansing to the afflicted.

Some have experienced a new dimension of power in prayer. They have come forth stronger, with a new determination to ride above the storms of life. They have experienced, through prayer, a touch of power and have found for themselves a new capability to cope with new situations in the strength of the Holy Spirit. Prayer restores!

2. Prayer Revives

The second word that is significant in the ministry of prayer is the word 'raise'. James says that *'the Lord will raise*' the sick. The word 'raise' comes from the Greek which can also be translated to mean 'to awaken' or 'to lift a person up from an infirmity'. The counsellee through the ministry of prayer is awakened to a new hope. He experiences a new day in his life. He is made to approach life from a positive viewpoint instead of a negative one. It lifts the counsellee from his position of defeat into the calm of God's love. He is revived. He experiences new meaning in his life.

3. *Prayer Cleanses*

The third word that is significant in the ministry of prayer is the word *'forgiven'*. James says, *'...if they have committed sins, they will be forgiven.'* Many counsellees come to the counsellor with an overwhelming sense of guilt. He needs to be freed from his guilt in order to receive wholeness of mind and spirit.

The counsellee comes with a need to receive forgiveness. He needs to know that God can forgive and will forgive. Of course there must be confession as a prelude to forgiveness. James in verse 16 says, *'Therefore, confess your sins to one another, and pray for one another, so that you may be healed.'* Christian counselling offers the counsellee the opportunity to confess his faults before the Lord in the presence of a counsellor. The Christian counsellor then ministers God's word of forgiveness through the avenue of prayer. The counsellee receives the forgiveness and is healed. Praise the Lord!

The Prayer Fellowship

The ministry of prayer is not only the work of the counsellor. James speaks of the special place Church Elders have in the ministry of prayer. He says, *'Is anyone among you sick? Let him call for the elders of the church, and let them pray over him'* (James 5:14). It is a desirable practice for counsellors to bring their counsellees to church elders for prayer as this underscores the fact that the ministry of prayer and counselling is church-based. The elders being mature, would inspire counsellees toward a closer relationship with the Lord.

Offering a Prayer

When do we offer prayer in the counselling process? There are no rules as to when prayer should be offered in the ministry process. Sometimes prayer can be offered just before the session begins or at the end of each session. Unless the counsellee is negative towards prayer, the ministry of prayer remains an important part of the counselling procedure.

Counsellors can usher their counsellees into the very presence of God in a ministry of prayer. Whilst counsellors can pray for their counsellees in their absence, there is a special place for a one-to-one prayer session with the counsellee. We offer intercessory prayer for counsellees with their consent. Apart from praying for God's guidance and direction to the counsellee, there are many things we can pray for including the Lord's protection, healing and comfort.

Prayers offered during counselling sessions can be soothing and comforting for the counsellee as he experiences an uplifting of his spirit in the presence of God. Sometimes a release takes place and the counsellee breaks down in tears of repentance and joy. Prayer is also offered as an acknowledgement of the centrality of Christ in the counselling encounter.

What About Ministering in Tongues?

Those with the gift of tongues should be cautious in the exercise of the gift while counselling. Whilst the gift can be used to the advantage of the counsellor it can also be a source of confusion for the uninformed. A counsellor should be careful not to use the prayer language of tongues while ministering to non-Christians. This would not only frighten them but also raise other unnecessary questions in their already confused minds.

The gift of tongues however can be appropriately used as a prayer language when ministering to a Christian. This is especially so when we have been praying for the counsellee in our known language and the need for a more intensive prayer ministry is evident. In such a case, the counsellee must be told that prayers would be offered in the language of the Spirit. We need to explain to the counsellee that the prayers offered in the language of the Spirit may not be understood by him, but that God does understand and will minister as we intercede. In many instances, the counsellees whom we have ministered to through this means have received comfort and have been blessed. Was it not Paul who said, *'the Spirit also helps our weaknesses; for we do not know how to pray as we should, but the Spirit Himself intercedes for us with groanings too deep for words; and He who searches the hearts knows what the mind of the Spirit is, because He intercedes for the saints according to the will of God'* (Romans 8:26–27). As we pray in the spirit, the Spirit prays on our behalf to God.

Group Prayer

There is also the place for group prayer. Sometimes when the counsellor feels a need for prayer support, he can turn to his prayer group to pray for him. To keep confidence, it may not be necessary for the group to know about the problem of the counsellee but the group can pray for wisdom for the counsellor and comfort and release for the counsellee. Sometimes, the counsellee might ask for prayers and if the counsellee has no objection that the prayer group prays for him by name, then this could be made known and the prayer group can give support as the counsellor engages in counselling. Some Christians may feel called to meet regularly to pray for the ministry of counselling in general.

Is it not wonderful to know that as we minister the comfort of Jesus, it is not only we who are praying, but there are also others who are praying for us?

Chapter 9

A Ministry of the Word

One of the questions that has been frequently asked by Christian counsellors is the use of the Bible in counselling. How can we use the Bible effectively in counselling? When should the counsellor refer to Scripture? When is it inappropriate to refer to Scripture?

In order for the Bible to be used effectively in the counselling process, the Christian counsellor must himself first be familiar with Scripture. It is imperative therefore for a counsellor to spend time studying the Word so that God can bring to the counsellor's memory passages of Scripture that he has read which would be of help in his counselling encounters. Even if passages of Scripture are not directly quoted, it is necessary for guidance on general scriptural directives to be shared.

We believe that the Bible is a powerful tool in counselling. The writer of the Book of Hebrews affirms this when he says, *'For the word of God is living and active and sharper than any two-edged sword, and piercing as far as the division of soul and spirit, of joints and marrow and able to judge the thoughts and intentions of the heart'* (Hebrews 4:12).

The Word of God is Living and Active

The first thing we note from Hebrews 12:4 is the fact that the Word of God is living and active. This alludes to the fact that the Bible is not a static dead entity, but a dynamic life-renewing Word. Because the Bible is living and active, it can in itself draw persons to God. We remember hearing the testimony of someone who came to know the Lord just by reading a Bible he found in a hotel room.

If the Bible is living and active, and if it can be used to draw persons to God, then it becomes an important counselling tool for the counsellor.

The Piercing Quality of the Word

The second quality of the Word of God is its ability, like a sharp two-edged sword, to pierce into the very soul of a person, bringing the counsellee to repentance and wholeness in Christ Jesus. If we believe that the Bible is the Word of God, then we must believe that God can speak through His written word as well. It has been our joy seeing counsellees blessed as we shared God's Word with them.

How Do We Use Scriptures?

Some ask the question as to whether we need to have our Bibles with us whenever we counsel. We do not think it is necessary for us always to have the Bible with us when we counsel, but we neeed to know what the Bible is saying concerning various issues of life and to use these as guiding principles in the counselling process.

Reading aloud from the Bible itself can be a help if the counsellee desires to know the source of a certain biblical truth or ethical viewpoint. This enables the counsellee to hear for himself what the Bible is saying concerning a particular issue that may be troubling him.

We have found the use of Scripture most effective in counselling the troubled and dying. The Words of Scripture have been a tremendous source of comfort and help to these persons.

We have, however, found it necessary to be discerning in the use of Scripture with sinning Christians. As they are familiar with Scripture and are conscious of their backsliding condition, they resent counsellors throwing Bible verses at them. For this reason, it is necessary for Christian counsellors to be wise in the use of Scripture so that counsellees can feel comfortable turning to counsellors for help.

Biblical Passages on Various Life Issues

Below are Biblical passages that may be of assistance to the Christian counsellor as he handles various issues in life.

Adultery

Exodus 20:14

> [14] *You shall not commit adultery.*

Proverbs 6:24–29, 32–33

> [24] *To keep you from the evil woman,*
> *From the smooth tongue of the adulteress.*
> [25] *Do not desire her beauty in your heart, Nor let her catch you with her eyelids.*
> [26] *For on account of a harlot one is reduced to a loaf of bread,*
> *And an adulteress hunts for the precious life.*
> [27] *Can a man take fire in his bosom,*
> *And his clothes not be burned?*
> [28] *Or can a man walk on hot coals,*
> *And his feet not be scorched?*
> [29] *So is the one who goes in to his neighbour's wife;*
> *Whoever touches her will not go unpunished.*
> [32] *The one who commits adultery with a woman is lacking sense;*
> *He who would destroy himself does it.*

³³ *Wounds and disgrace he will find,*
  And his reproach will not be blotted out.

Matthew 5:27–28

²⁷ *You have heard that it was said, 'You shall not commit adultery';*
²⁸ *But I say to you, that everyone who looks on a woman to lust for her has committed adultery with her already in his heart.*

Affliction

Job 5:6–7

⁶ *For affliction does not come from the dust,*
  Neither does trouble sprout from the ground,
⁷ *For man is born for trouble,*
  As sparks fly upward.

Job 5:17–18

¹⁷ *Behold, how happy is the man whom God reproves,*
  So do not despise the discipline of the Almighty.
¹⁸ *For He inflicts pain, and gives relief;*
  He wounds, and His hands also heal.

Psalm 50:15

¹⁵ *And call upon Me in the day of trouble;*
  I will rescue you, and you will honour Me.

Matthew 11:28

²⁸ *Come to Me, all who are weary and heavy-laden, and I will give you rest.*

Romans 5:3–4

³ *And not only this, but we also exult in our tribulations, knowing that tribulation brings about perseverance;*
⁴ *and perserverance, proven character, and proven character, hope.*

Alcoholism

Proverbs 20:1

> [1] *Wine is a mocker, strong drink a brawler, And whoever is intoxicated by it is not wise.*

Proverbs 23:29–33

> [29] *Who has woe? Who has sorrow? Who has contentions? Who has complaining? Who has wounds without cause? Who has redness of eyes?*
> [30] *Those who linger long over wine,*
> *Those who go to taste mixed wine.*
> [31] *Do not look on the wine when it is red, When it sparkles in the cup, When it goes down smoothly;*
> [32] *At last it bites like a serpent,*
> *And stings like a viper.*
> [33] *Your eyes will see strange things,*
> *And your mind will utter perverse things.*

Isaiah 5:11–12, 22

> [11] *Woe to those who rise early in the morning that they may pursue strong drink; who stay up late in the evening that wine may inflame them!*
> [12] *And their banquets are accompanied by lyre and harp, by tambourine and flute, and by wine;*
> *But they do not pay attention to the deeds of the LORD,*
> *Nor do they consider the work of His hands.*
> [22] *Woe to those who are heroes in drinking wine,*
> *And valiant men in mixing strong drink.*

Ephesians 5:18

> [18] *And do not get drunk with wine, for that is dissipation, but be filled with the Spirit.*

Anger

Psalm 37:8–9

> [8] *Cease from anger and forsake wrath;*
> *Do not fret, it leads only to evildoing.*
> [9] *For evildoers will be cut off,*
> *But those who wait for the Lord, they will inherit the land.*

Proverbs 14:17

> [17] *A quick-tempered man acts foolishly . . .*

Ephesians 4:26–27

> [26] *Be angry,* **and** *yet do not sin; do not let the sun go down on your anger,*
> [27] *and do not give the devil an opportunity.*

Colossians 3:8

> [8] *But now you also, put them all aside: anger, wrath, malice, slander, and abusive speech from your mouth.*

James 1:19–20

> [19] *This you know, my beloved brethren. But let everyone be quick to hear, slow to speak and slow to anger;*
> [20] *for the anger of man does not achieve the righteousness of God.*

Anxiety

Psalm 37:5

> [5] *Commit your way to the LORD,*
> *Trust also in Him, and He will do it.*

Matthew 6:25–34

> [25] *For this reason I say to you, do not be anxious for your life, as to what you shall eat, or what you shall drink; nor for your body, as to what you shall put on. Is not life more than food, and the body than clothing?*

26 *Look at the birds of the air, that they do not sow, neither do they reap, nor gather into barns, and yet your heavenly Father feeds them. Are you not worth much more than they?*

27 *And which of you by being anxious can add a single cubit to his life's span?*

28 *And why are you anxious about clothing? Observe how the lilies of the field grow; they do not toil, nor do they spin,*

29 *yet I say to you that even Solomon in all his glory did not clothe himself like one of these.*

30 *But if God so arrays the grass of the field, which is alive today and tomorrow is thrown into the furnace, will He not much more do so for you, O men of little faith?*

31 *Do not be anxious then saying, 'What shall we eat?' or 'What shall we drink?' or 'With what shall we clothe ourselves?'*

32 *For all these things the Gentiles eagerly seek; for your heavenly Father knows that you need all these things.*

33 *But seek first His kingdom and His righteousness; and all these things shall be added to you.*

34 *Therefore do not be anxious for tomorrow; for tomorrow will care for itself. Each day has enough trouble of its own.*

Luke 21:34

34 *Be on guard, that your hearts may not be weighted down with dissipation and drunkenness and the worries of life, and that day come on you suddenly like a trap.*

Philippians 4:6–7

6 *Be anxious for nothing, but in everything by prayer and supplication with thanksgiving let your requests be made known to God.*

7 *And the peace of God, which surpasses all com-
prehension, shall guard your hearts and your minds in
Christ Jesus.*

1 Peter 5:6–7

6 *Humble yourselves, therefore under the mighty hand
of God that He may exalt you at the proper time,*

7 *casting all your anxiety upon Him, because He cares
for you.*

Bereavement

John 11:25–26

25 *Jesus said to her, 'I am the resurrection and the life; he
who believes in Me shall live even if he dies,*

26 *and everyone who lives and believes in Me shall never
die. Do you believe this?'*

John 14:1–6

1 *'Let not your heart be troubled; believe in God,
believe also in Me.*

2 *In My Father's house are many dwelling places; if it
were not so, I would have told you; for I go to prepare
a place for you.*

3 *And if I go and prepare a place for you, I will come
again and receive you to Myself; that where I am, there
you may be also.*

4 *And you know the way where I am going.'*

5 *Thomas said to Him, 'Lord, we do not know where
You are going, how do we know the way?'*

6 *Jesus said to him, 'I am the way, and the truth, and the
life; no one comes to the Father, but through Me.'*

1 Corinthians 15:55–57

55 *'O death, where is your victory? O death, where is
your sting?'*

56 *The sting of death is sin, and the power of sin is the
law;*

57 *but thanks be to God, who gives us the victory through our Lord Jesus Christ.*

2 Corinthians 5:1

1 *For we know that if the earthly tent which is our house is torn down, we have a building from God, a house not made with hands eternal in the heavens.*

Revelation 21:2–4

2 *And I saw the holy city, new Jerusalem, coming down out of heaven from God, made ready as a bride adorned for her husband.*

3 *And I heard a loud voice from the throne, saying, 'Behold, the tabernacle of God is among men, and He shall dwell among them, and they shall be His people, and God Himself shall be among them,*

4 *and He shall wipe away every tear from their eyes; and there shall no longer be any death; there shall no longer be any mourning, or crying or pain; . . .'*

Bitterness and Hatred

Psalm 66:18

18 *If I regard wickedness in my heart,*
The Lord will not hear.

Matthew 5:43–44

43 *You have heard that it was said, 'You shall love your neighbour, and hate your enemy.'*

44 *But I say to you, love your enemies, and pray for those who persecute you . . .*

Ephesians 4:31–32

31 *Let all bitterness and wrath and anger and clamour and slander be put away from you, along with all malice.*

32 *And be kind to one another, tender-hearted, forgiving each other, just as God in Christ also has forgiven you.*

Hebrews 12:14–15

> [14] *Pursue peace with all men, and the sanctification without which no one will see the Lord.*
> [15] *See to it that no one comes short of the grace of God; that no root of bitterness springing up causes trouble, and by it many be defiled...*

1 John 3:15

> [15] *Everyone who hates his brother is a murderer; and you know that no murderer has eternal life abiding in him.*

Demonic Influence

James 4:7

> [7] *Submit therefore to God. Resist the devil and he will flee from you.*

1 Peter 5:8–9

> [8] *Be of sober spirit, be on the alert. Your adversary, the devil, prowls about like a roaring lion, seeking someone to devour.*
> [9] *But resist him, firm in your faith, knowing that the same experiences of suffering are being accomplished by your brethren who are in the world.*
> [10] *And after you have suffered for a little while, the God of all grace, who called you to His eternal glory in Christ, will Himself perfect, confirm, strengthen and establish you.*

1 John 4:1–4

> [1] *Beloved, do not believe every spirit, but test the spirits to see whether they are from God; because many false prophets have gone out into the world.*
> [2] *By this you know the Spirit of God; every spirit that confesses that Jesus Christ has come in the flesh is from God;*

> [3] *and every spirit that does not confess Jesus is not from God; and this is the spirit of the antichrist, of which you have heard that it is coming, and now it is already in the world.*
> [4] *You are from God, little children, and have overcome them; because greater is He who is in you than he who is in the world.*

Depressed

John 14:27

> [27] *Peace I leave with you; My peace I give to you; not as the world gives, do I give to you. Let not your heart be troubled, nor let it be fearful.*

Divorce

Matthew 5:31–32

> [31] *And it was said, 'Whoever divorces his wife, let him give her a certificate of dismissal';*
> [32] *But I say to you that everyone who divorces his wife, except for the cause of unchastity, makes her commit adultery; and whoever marries a divorced woman commits adultery.*

Matthew 19:9

> [9] *And I say to you, whoever divorces his wife except for immorality, and marries another woman commits adultery.*

Envy

Psalm 37:1

> [1] *Fret not yourself because of evildoers,*
> *Be not envious towards wrongdoers.*

Proverbs 23:17

> [17] *Do not let your heart envy sinners, But live in the fear of the Lord always.*

Galatians 5:19–21

> ¹⁹ *Now the deeds of the flesh are evident, which are: immorality, impurity, sensuality,*
> ²⁰ *idolatry, sorcery, enmities, strife, jealousy, outbursts of anger, disputes, dissensions, factions,*
> ²¹ *envyings, drunkenness, carousings, and things like these, of which I forewarn you just as I have forewarned that those who practise such things shall not inherit the kingdom of God.*

Faithfulness (Fidelity)

Proverbs 5:18–21

> ¹⁸ *Let your fountain be blessed,*
> *And rejoice in the wife of your youth.*
> ¹⁹ *As a loving hind and a graceful doe,*
> *Let her breasts satisfy you at all times;*
> *Be exhilarated always with her love.*
> ²⁰ *For why should you, my son be exhilarated with an adulteress,*
> *And embrace the bosom of a foreigner?*
> ²¹ *For the ways of a man are before the eyes of the Lord,*
> *And He watches all his paths.*

Fear

Psalm 27:1

> ¹ *The Lord is my light and my salvation;*
> *Whom shall I fear?*
> *The Lord is the defence of my life;*
> *Whom shall I dread?*

Psalm 55:4–6, 22

> ⁴ *My heart is in anguish within me,*
> *And the terrors of death have fallen upon me.*
> ⁵ *Fear and trembling come upon me;*
> *And horror has overwhelmed me.*

⁶ *And I said, 'Oh that I had wings like a dove! I would*
fly away and be at rest.'
²² *Cast your burden upon the* LORD, *and He will sustain*
you;
He will never allow the righteous to be shaken.

Isaiah 41:10–13

¹⁰ *Do not fear, for I am with you;*
Do not anxiously look about you for I am your God.
I will strengthen you, surely I will help you,
Surely I will uphold you with My righteous right hand.
¹¹ *Behold, all those who are angered at you will be*
shamed and dishonoured;
Those who contend with you will be as nothing, and
will perish.
¹² *You will seek those who quarrel with you, but will not*
find them, those who war with you will be as nothing,
and non-existent.
¹³ *For I am the Lord your God, who upholds your right*
hand, Who says to you, 'Do not fear, I will help you.'

Romans 8:15

¹⁵ *For you have not received a spirit of slavery leading to*
fear again, but you have received a spirit of adoption
as sons by which we cry out, 'Abba! Father!'

2 Timothy 1:7

⁷ *For God has not given us a spirit of timidity, but of*
power and love and discipline.

1 John 4:18

¹⁸ *There is no fear in love; but perfect love casts out fear,*
because fear involves punishment, and the one who
fears is not perfected in love.

Guilt

John 8:36

> ³⁶ *If therefore the Son shall make you free, you shall be free indeed.*

2 Corinthians 5:17

> ¹⁷ *Therefore if any man is in Christ, He is a new creature; the old things passed away; behold, new things have come.*

Isaiah 43:25

> ²⁵ *I, even I, am the one who wipes out your transgressions for My own sake;*
> *And I will not remember your sins.*

Healing

Psalm 147:3

> ³ *He heals the brokenhearted,*
> *And binds up their wounds.*

Jeremiah 17:14

> ¹⁴ *Heal me, O LORD, and I will be healed; Save me and I will be saved,*
> *For Thou are my praise.*

Matthew 10:1

> ¹ *And having summoned His twelve disciples, He gave them authority over unclean spirits, to cast them out, and to heal every kind of disease and every kind of sickness.*

James 5:14–15

> ¹⁴ *Is anyone among you sick? Let him call the elders of the church, and let them pray over him, anointing him with oil in the name of the Lord;*

¹⁵ *and the prayer offered in faith will restore the one who is sick, and the Lord will raise Him up, and if he has committed sins, they will be forgiven him.*

Homosexuals

1 Corinthians 6:9–10

⁹ *Or do you not know that the unrighteous shall not inherit the kingdom of God? Do not be deceived; neither fornicators, nor idolaters, nor adulterers, nor effeminate, nor homosexuals,*
¹⁰ *nor thieves, nor the covetous, nor drunkards, nor revilers, nor swindlers, shall inherit the kingdom of God.*

1 Timothy 1:9–10

⁹ *Realizing the fact that law is not made for a righteous man, but for those who are lawless and rebellious, for the unholy and profane, for those who kill their fathers or mothers, for murderers*
¹⁰ *and immoral men and homosexuals and kidnappers and liars and perjurers, and whatever else is contrary to sound teaching.*

Hope

Psalm 71:5

⁵ *For Thou art my hope;*
O Lord GOD, Thou art my confidence from my youth

Jeremiah 17:7

⁷ *Blessed is the man who trusts in the LORD And whose trust is the LORD.*

Romans 8:24–25

²⁴ *For in hope we have been saved, but hope that is seen is not hope; for why does one hope for what he sees?*

25 *But if we hope for what we do not see, with per-severance we wait eagerly for it.*

Insecurity

Romans 8:38:39

38 *For I am convinced that neither death, nor life, nor angels, nor principalities, nor things present, nor things to come, nor powers,*

39 *nor height, nor depth, nor any other created thing, shall be able to separate us from the love of God, which is in Christ Jesus our Lord.*

1 Timothy 6:17–19

17 *Instruct those who are rich in this present world not to be conceited or to fix their hope on the uncertainty of riches, but on God, who richly supplies us with all things to enjoy.*

18 *Instruct them to do good, to be rich in good works, to be generous and ready to share,*

19 *storing up for themselves the treasure of a good foundation for the future, so that they may take hold of that which is life indeed.*

Hebrews 13:5–6

5 *Let your character be free from the love of money, being content with what you have; for He Himself has said, 'I will never desert you, nor will I ever forsake you,'*

6 *so that we confidently say, 'The Lord is my helper, I will not be afraid. What shall man do to me?'*

Psalm 23

1 *The LORD is my shepherd,*
I shall not want.
2 *He makes me lie down in green pastures;*
He leads me beside quiet waters.

³ *He restores my soul;*
  He guides me in the paths of righteousness for His
  name's sake.
⁴ *Even though I walk through the valley of shadow of*
  death, I fear no evil; for Thou art with me;
  Thy rod and Thy staff, they comfort me.
⁵ *Thou dost prepare a table before me in the presence of*
  mine enemies;
  Thou has anointed my head with oil;
  My cup overflows.
⁶ *Surely goodness and loving-kindness will follow me*
  all the days of my life, and I dwell in the house of the
  LORD forever.

Psalm 118:5–9

⁵ *From my distress I called upon the LORD;*
  The LORD answered me and set me in a large place.
⁶ *The LORD is for me; I will not fear;*
  What can man do to me?
⁷ *The LORD is for me among those who help me;*
  Therefore I shall look with satisfaction on those who
  hate me.
⁸ *It is better to take refuge in the LORD*
  Than to trust in man.
⁹ *It is better to take refuge in the LORD*
  Than to trust in princes.

Marriage

Genesis 2:23–24

²³ *And the man said, 'This is now bone of my bones,*
  And flesh of my flesh; She shall be called Woman,
  Because she was taken out of Man.'
²⁴ *For this cause a man shall leave his father and his*
  mother, and shall cleave to his wife; and they shall
  become one flesh.

1 Corinthians 11:11–12

> [11] *However, in the Lord, neither is woman independent of man, nor is man independent of woman.*
> [12] *For as the woman originates from the man, so also the man has his birth through the woman; and all things originate from God.*

Pessimism

Philippians 4:8

> [8] *Finally, brethren, whatever is true, whatever is honourable, whatever is right, whatever is pure, whatever is lovely, whatever is of good repute, if there is any excellence and if anything worthy of praise, let your mind dwell on these things.*

Philippians 4:13

> [13] *I can do all things through Him who strengthens me.*

Rejection

Psalm 68:5–6

> [5] *A father of the fatherless and a judge for the widows, Is God in His holy habitations.*
> [6] *God makes a home for the lonely; He leads out the prisoners into prosperity, only the rebellious dwell in a parched land.*

Psalm 139:17–18

> [17] *How precious also are Thy thoughts to me, O God! How vast is the sum of them!*
> [18] *If I should count them, they would outnumber the sand. When I awake, I am still with Thee.*

Repentance

2 Chronicles 7:14

> ¹⁴*And if My people who are called by My name humble themselves and pray, and seek My face and turn from their wicked ways, then I will hear from heaven, will forgive their sins, and will heal their land.*

Isaiah 55:6–7

> ⁶*Seek the LORD while He may be found;*
> *Call upon Him while He is near.*
> ⁷*Let the wicked forsake his way,*
> *And the unrighteous man his thoughts;*
> *And let him return to the LORD,*
> *And He will have compassion on him;*
> *And to our God,*
> *For He will abundantly pardon.*

Acts 3:19

> ¹⁹*Repent therefore and return, that your sins may be wiped away, in order that times of refreshing may come from the presence of the Lord.*

1 John 1:9

> ⁹*If we confess our sins, He is faithful and righteous to forgive us our sins and cleanse us from all unrighteousness.*

Suffering

Romans 8:18

> ¹⁸*For I consider that the sufferings of this present time are not worthy to be compared with the glory that is to be revealed to us.*

Romans 8:28

> ²⁸*And we know that God causes all things to work together for good to those who love God, to those who are called according to His purpose.*

Romans 8:35, 37

> 35 *Who shall separate us from the love of Christ? Shall tribulation, or distress, or persecution, or famine, or nakedness, or peril or sword?*
>
> 37 *But in all these things we overwhelmingly conquer through Him who loved us.*

Temptation

Proverbs 1:10

> 10 *My son, if sinners entice you,*
>   *Do not consent.*

Proverbs 4:14–15

> 14 *Do not enter the path of the wicked,*
>   *And do not proceed in the way of the evil men.*
>
> 15 *Avoid it, do not pass by it;*
>   *Turn away from it and pass on.*

Matthew 26:41

> 41 *Keep watching and praying, that you may not enter into temptation; the spirit is willing, but the flesh is weak.*

1 Corinthians 10:13

> 13 *No temptation has overtaken you but such as is common to man; and God is faithful, who will not allow you to be tempted beyond what you are able, but with the temptation will provide the way to escape also, that you may be able to endure it.*

Unforgiveness

Matthew 6:14–15

> 14 *For if you forgive men for their transgressions, your heavenly Father will also forgive you.*
>
> 15 *But if you do not forgive men, then your Father will not forgive your transgressions.*

Mark 11:25

> [25] *And whenever you stand praying, forgive, if you have anything against anyone; so that your Father also who is in heaven may forgive you your transgressions.*

Ephesians 4:32

> [32] *And be kind to one another, tender-hearted, forgiving each other, just as God in Christ also has forgiven you.*

Vengeance

Romans 12:19

> [19] *Never take your own revenge, beloved, but leave room for the wrath of God, for it is written, 'Vengeance is Mine, I will repay,' says the Lord.*

Chapter 10

A Spirit-Filled Counsellor

Sharing our lives in Christian ministry demands more than our natural abilities. We cannot rely on our intelligence or resources alone to do God's work. Our own skills and abilities have their limitations. Our dependence in Christian ministry must always be on the Lord. Supernatural results can only be attained through supernatural assistance.

The wonderful legacy that we have as Christians is Jesus' departing gift in the person of the Holy Spirit. He said, *'And I will ask the Father, and He will give you another Helper (Counsellor, Comforter) that He may be with you forever'* (John 14:16).[1] The early disciples never fully understood the breadth of this promise until the Holy Spirit fell upon them at Pentecost and empowered them as His witnesses to the ends of the earth.

The Gift of the Holy Spirit

The Holy Spirit is the Counsellor of counsellors. He, like Jesus, is the Wonderful Counsellor. Jesus said that He would send 'another Helper' or 'another Counsellor'. If the Holy Spirit is the other Counsellor, then in every way He is like Jesus who is the first Counsellor. But because He is Spirit, He has the advantage of being anywhere and everywhere at the same time. Many lives have been touched through the work of the Holy Spirit and many more will experience renewal as Christian counsellors guided by the Holy Spirit perform their God-given task of caring and comforting.

We remember the words of Jesus in Acts 1:8 when He said, *'You shall receive power when the Holy Spirit has come upon you; and you shall be My witnesses both in Jerusalem, and in all Judea and Samaria, and even to the remotest parts of the earth.'* The purpose of empowerment as we see in this passage is in order that we may be His witnesses.

We believe that Christian counselling serves as an avenue of Christian witness. We serve as Christ's witnesses through the ministry of care and counselling. Whenever lives are touched by the ministry of love, people become receptive to the message of the gospel. People receive Christ through the ministry of Christian counselling because they see reflected in the Christian counsellor the person of Jesus Christ. God, as he empowers us to witness through the ministry of counselling, allows us ample opportunities to share the gospel with our counsellees.

The Baptism in the Holy Spirit and the Christian Counsellor

Whilst anyone can be engaged in counselling, the Christian counsellor who desires to be effective needs to be baptized in the Holy Spirit. As Christian counselling is God-directed counselling, it is imperative that the counsellee be filled with the Spirit of God.

In recent times, many have been confused by the concept of the baptism in the Holy Spirit. Some have equated the baptism in the Holy Spirit with speaking in tongues while others talk about baptism in the Holy Spirit as synonymous with the entry of the Holy Spirit into a person's life at the time of conversion. We feel that it is quite unnecessary to argue as to when a person is baptized in the Holy Spirit because when that takes place a person knows it and those around him would also notice it. A person who is baptized in the Holy Spirit knows that the Spirit indwells him to empower him for witnessing.

The baptism in the Holy Spirit is a life-transforming experience. It is basically the baptism of power for the purpose of witness. It creates such a change in a person's life that he desires only to please the Lord and do that which will glorify His name. To be baptized in the Holy Spirit is not synonymous with speaking in tongues, although it is not unusual for a person who is baptized in the Holy Spirit also to speak in tongues. A person who is baptized in the Holy Spirit avails himself to all the gifts of the Holy Spirit that may be bestowed upon him including the gift of tongues. He seeks from God all the gifts that will make him effective as a Christian witness.

To be baptized in the Holy Spirit is to be filled with the Holy Spirit; it is to be completely immersed in the Holy Spirit both within and without. It is not only having the Holy Spirit but also being possessed by Him. The evidence of the Spirit's baptism is manifested in a life of power. It is not having power for its own sake, but power for the work of ministry. It is receiving power for service. Christian counsellors need to lead Spirit-empowered lives if they are to be effective in the work of counselling.

The Christian counsellor can receive baptism in the Holy Spirit through prayer as he invites the Holy Spirit to take complete control of his life. It is in the daily yielding and submission of the counsellor's life to the Holy Spirit that he becomes increasingly sensitized to His promptings and is enabled to minister as led by the Spirit. He can also receive the baptism in the Holy Spirit through the laying on of hands by his pastor or elders of the church (Acts 19:6).

In our ministry of counselling, we have always felt the need of the Spirit's presence. We have sought the Spirit's aid to assist us in our various encounters. He has helped us in our interviews with counsellees; He has helped us in discerning the felt needs of others; He has helped us express compassion and care in ways that counsellees can respond to. We praise God for that.

The Fruit of the Spirit and the Christian Counsellor

As Christian counsellors, our lives and countenances need to reflect the radiance of Christ. We are not suggesting that we wear masks of radiance; we are saying that the joy and peace of the Lord in our lives can be real and spontaneous. If we believe that inner healing is a reality, then we too can experience the touch of Jesus and manifest the fruit of the Spirit which is the consequent manifestation of a Christian who has been healed and empowered by the Lord.

Counsellees respond well to counsellors who themselves know the joy of being released from the power of sin and who in their lives portray qualities of gentleness and compassion. Paul understood this when he said that *'the fruit of the Spirit is love, joy, peace, patience, kindness, goodness, faithfulness, gentleness, self-control; against such things there is no law'* (Galatians 5:22–23). Some scholars are of the opinion that the passage should be read thus, 'the fruit of the Spirit is love – joy, peace, patience, kindness, goodness, faithfulness, gentleness, self-control.' We go along with this interpretation where the one fruit of the Spirit is love. The rest that follow such as joy, peace, patience, kindness, goodness, faithfulness, gentleness, and self-control are but manifestations or characteristics of love. In other words, if we have love we also have the accompanying attributes of joy, peace, patience, kindness and the like.

This is affirmed by Paul in his dialogue on love found in 1 Corinthians 13. He says,

Love is patient
Love is kind
Love is not jealous
Love does not brag
Love is not arrogant
Love does not act unbecomingly
Love is not provoked
Love does not take into account a wrong suffered
Love does not rejoice in unrighteousness
Love rejoices with the truth
Love bears all things
Love believes all things
Love hopes all things
Love endures all things.

It is interesting to note that the Greek word used to describe love in 1 Corinthians 13 is the word *agape*. The word expresses a love that is unconditional and unselfish. It is a love that is willing to go the second mile for the sake of others. It is a quality of love that has foundation in God Himself – *'for God so loved the world that He gave...'* (John 3:16). God's love is all-giving. We are called to radiate the same love in our ministry of comfort and care.

Following the passage in Galatians 5, Paul continues his discussion on the Spirit-life by saying, *'Brethren, even if a man is caught in any trespass, you who are spiritual, restore such a one in a spirit of gentleness; each one looking to yourself, lest you too be tempted. Bear one another's burdens, and thus fulfil the law of Christ'* (Galatians 6:1–2).

Paul in his letter to the churches in Galatia, recognizes the importance of compassion. He comments that the nature of man is such as to lead him to transgress the laws of God. Yet, Paul also stresses that under the conviction of the Holy Spirit, such a person can find restoration and reconciliation with the Lord. This can best be done in the spirit of gentleness.

Paul comments on the frailty of man and how easily he

can fall into temptation. As such, ministry to a fallen brethren should not be one of arrogance but one of gentleness and care. Paul calls for mutual support and encouragement in the Body of Christ in the words, *'Bear one another's burdens, and thus fulfil the law of Christ.'* As we submit ourselves in full dependence on the Holy Spirit, the expressions of the fruit of the Spirit can be released in our lives to the glory of God.

The Anointing of the Holy Spirit and the Christian Counsellor

Christian counsellors need to ask for the Lord's anointing in their ministry. Jesus began His ministry by saying, *'The Spirit of the Lord is upon me, because He anointed me...'* If Jesus the Son of God needed to be anointed to minister, we too need the same anointing.

To be anointed is to be enabled to serve. It is to receive the enabling of the Holy Spirit for ministry. The Holy Spirit comes as the anointing oil upon us. As the Holy Spirit was poured upon Christ and upon the Church at Pentecost, He must be poured over us if we are to receive unction in ministry. The Apostle John says, *'And as for you, the anointing which you received from Him abides in you, and you have no need for anyone to teach you; but as His anointing teaches you about all things, and is true and not a lie, and just as it has taught you, you abide in Him'* (1 John 2:27).

There are two things that we can draw from 1 John 2:27 about the anointing.

Firstly, the anointing is abiding. It abides in you. When a person receives the anointing, he becomes constantly aware of the abiding presence of the Holy Spirit in his life. He knows that the Holy Spirit is there to guide him in the work of ministry. For the Christian counsellor, he can rest assured that the Holy Spirit is there to grant him wisdom in his counselling ministry.

The second thing we can draw from 1 John 2:27 is that the anointed counsellor receives his teaching from the Holy Spirit. The Holy Spirit becomes the counsellor's personal tutor. The Holy Spirit instructs the counsellor what he should do at every juncture of the counselling process. He becomes effective because of divine instruction. This does not mean that the counsellor avoids the discipline of academic work or the need for instruction, it means that the Holy Spirit imbues the Christian counsellor with wisdom and specific direction.

The Truth Sets us Free

If the Christian counsellor is to be effective in his ministry of counselling, he must know the truth about his counsellee. It is in this realm that the Christian counsellor seeks the enabling of the Holy Spirit because He is the Spirit of Truth. He guides both the counsellee and the counsellor into all truth.

In counselling, truthfulness is an essential ingredient. The counsellee should tell the truth, and the counsellor should know the truth so that he can minister effectively. Jesus says, *'when He, the Spirit of Truth comes, He will guide you into all truth'* (John 16:13). The Holy Spirit can guide the counsellor and the counsellee into all truth. Whilst the counsellor needs to know the truth to assist the counsellee, the counsellee needs to know the truth about himself in order to receive wholeness of mind and spirit. Christ's injunction to us is to know the truth about God and ourselves (John 8:32). It is in knowing the truth that we are set completely free.

It is interesting to note that Jesus calls Himself *'the truth'* (John 14:6) and it is not by accident that Jesus refers to the Holy Spirit as *'the Spirit of truth'* (John 14:17). The Holy Trinity personifies truth. The integrity of the Triune God rests on this very attribute of Truth.

There are three ways in which the Holy Spirit functions as the Spirit of Truth.

Firstly, He causes the counsellee to see the truth about his situation. In many instances, counsellees in their attempt to rationalize their predicaments hide from the truth. They would rather live in an illusion than to know the truth because the knowledge of the truth is too painful for them to bear.

We once ministered to a counsellee who had a problem of guilt. He had undergone several sessions with a psychiatrist before coming to see us. As we discerned his problem, we asked if he had told the psychiatrist the real cause of his predicament. His answer was in the negative. When asked why he had not revealed the truth to the psychiatrist, his reply was that the former had never asked that of him. Whatever the reason, it was evident to us that he was not willing to deal with the truth.

In the counselling encounter, the Holy Spirit works through the counsellor, and enables the counsellee to see the truth about himself. It is as the counsellee recognises the truth and is willing to work out his situation on the basis of truth that he receives wholeness and release.

We once counselled a woman who could not see herself as the cause of her marital problems. It was only when she recognized the truth about herself that she could deal with her situation positively.

Secondly, the Holy Spirit helps the counsellor guide the counsellee in sharing the truth. The Holy Spirit grants the counsellor discernment in knowing if the counsellee is speaking the truth. He guides the counsellor and enables him to ask the right questions in order to ascertain the truth about the counsellee's situation.

Thirdly, the Holy Spirit enables the counsellor to discern truth even when the counsellee is unable to ascertain for himself the truth about his situation. The Christian counsellor is guided by the Holy Spirit into all truth. One of the assurances we have as Christian counsellors is the fact that when God calls us for a particular ministry, He also bestows upon us gifts suited for the task. The Holy Spirit who is the Counsellor, will bestow on us gifts that will enable us to be effective in our work of counselling.

The Gifts of the Holy Spirit and the Christian Counsellor

The Bible speaks of the variety of spiritual gifts available to the Christian counsellor (Romans 12:6–8; 1 Corinthians 12:7–11; Ephesians 4:11). Among the gifts of the Spirit the following stand out as being of immediate value to the Christian counsellor.

1. The Gift of Wisdom

The phrase that is used for the gift of wisdom in Scripture is the 'Word of Wisdom' (1 Corinthians 12:8) or in Greek the *logos sophias*. It has to do with the spoken word of wisdom as articulated by the counsellor in response to a particular situation. It is wisdom given by God in the handling of a particular situation. It is God's way of assisting the counsellor when faced with a difficult counselling situation. Wisdom is the truth of God revealed to man at a particular point and time for a particular purpose. It is a gift that God promises to a counsellor who would but ask in faith. In James 1:5–7, James says,

> 'If any of you lacks wisdom, let him ask God who gives to all men generously and without reproach, and it will be given him. But let him ask in faith without any doubting, for the one who doubts is like the surf of the sea driven and tossed by the wind. For let not that man expect that he will receive anything from the Lord.'

In our ministry, we have constantly found the need to turn to God for wisdom. We have found the promise of

James so true as the Lord has on every occasion granted us the wisdom necessary for each counselling situation.

King Solomon was given the Gift of Wisdom when he was called upon to sort out a dispute between two mothers over the ownership of an infant child. The story as recorded in 1 Kings 3:16–28 reflects the word of wisdom given by God to Solomon to sort out the problem. He was given the word of wisdom to help him ascertain who the rightful mother was. As Solomon needed wisdom in his ministry, we too need the wisdom from God as we encounter difficult counselling situations.

2. *The Gift of Knowledge*

The Gift of Knowledge is the *logos* of knowledge (1 Corinthians 12:8) given to Christians for the work of ministry. It is knowledge intellectually or supernaturally acquired. It is the God-given ability to absorb knowledge that is available in prevailing literature, or knowledge acquired through special revelation. The latter is well illustrated in Peter's encounter with Ananias and Sapphira who had cheated God. We are told from Acts 5 that Ananias and Sapphira had sold a piece of property with the intention of giving all the proceeds to God. Instead of doing that, they kept some of the proceeds and gave the rest to the apostles. Peter was upset when it was revealed to him through the word of knowledge that the couple had jointly cheated God. This led to Peter's rebuke upon the couple, and their subsequent demise.

Sometimes in the ministry of counselling, the word of knowledge is given to the counsellor by the Holy Spirit. This allows the counsellor to counsel in a certain direction in order to receive the best results. This is of special advantage for the Christian counsellor who needs to know the heart of the counsellee when he is engaged in counselling.

I (Isaac) remember a young man making an appointment to meet me. When he entered my office, the Lord revealed to me that this man had a homosexual problem. This was confirmed through the counselling interview. The gift of knowledge helps us in our ministry of comfort and care.

3. The Gift of Faith

The gift of faith (1 Corinthians 12:9) is another essential gift available for the Christian counsellor. It has nothing to do with 'saving' faith which is our response to God's offer of salvation. The gift of faith in Christian counselling is an intense belief that God is going to act in a particular counselling situation and restore the counsellee to wholeness and health. It is having an inexplicable confidence that God will intervene and that all will be well. The counsellor must come to God believing that He is sovereign and is in control of every situation. The writer of the book of Hebrews says, *'And without faith it is impossible to please Him, for he who comes to God must believe that He is, and that He is a rewarder of those who seek Him'* (Hebrews 11:6).

God acts when we believe. God acts when we trust Him completely. Jesus says, *'Truly I say to you, whoever says to this mountain, "Be taken up and cast into the sea," and does not doubt in his heart, but believes that what he says is going to happen, it shall be granted him. Therefore I say to you, all things for which you pray and ask, believe that you have received them, and they shall be granted you'* (Mark 11:23, 24).

The gift of faith allows the counsellor to minister with confidence knowing that the Lord will respond as he brings the counsellee before God's throne of grace.

4. The Gifts of Healing

The gift of healing is a plus for Christian counsellors who can exercise the gift. It is interesting to note that Paul in 1 Corinthians 12:9 uses the plural 'gifts' when referring to this spiritual gift. By implication, Paul is not talking about one gift of healing but several gifts of healing.

The Bible alludes to healings that are physical, psychological and spiritual. The Christian counsellor as he counsels can seek the Holy Spirit's anointing for a particular gift of healing, to meet a particular need. In many instances, the gift that is required most is the gift of inner healing. This enables the counsellee to experience a special unloading of his burdens at Calvary, and be released to praise the Lord.

Jennifer came to me (Shirley) for prayer and counselling when she was offered a top level post in a multi-national company. She was hand-picked for the job and her friends thought she would have no problem handling the work. However, Jennifer was apprehensive and entered into a period of depression. She was negative about herself and feared failure even before she began. Her usual confidence and positiveness simply vanished and even her physical appearance suffered a let-down. She grew thin and sloppy in her dressing. Her image had changed and she was terrified at what was happening. She would break down into tears so often that she feared she would not cope with life itself, let alone a new job.

As we prayed, the Lord began to heal Jennifer. It was an interesting sequence of events. Jennifer identified a basic fear she had since childhood. Jennifer's mother was a mistress to a rich businessman who had stolen time off quietly for many years to be with Jennifer and her mother. Jennifer loved her father dearly and had always feared for him, that his deception would one day be discovered. Fears such as this tormented Jennifer's childhood and she grew up feeling insecure. She could not trust many people and she was often suspicious even of her own husband. I discerned Jennifer's need for love and security and prayed for a healing of the damage caused in her troubled childhood. As Jennifer experienced release and inner healing, she was able to begin building up positive attitudes toward her new job. Having pulled out of the severe depression at an important time in her life, she exclaimed, 'Now I know

what it means to turn to Christ as the Great Physician.'
Healing is an important goal of Christian counselling.

5. *The Gift of Distinguishing of Spirits*

The word 'distinguishing' as found in 1 Corinthians 12:10
is the Greek *diakrisis* which can also be translated as
'discerning'. This gift of discernment is of special importance to the counsellor because it enables him to discern
the condition of the counsellee during the interview. This
gift is especially important when dealing with problems of
a demonic nature. The gift of distinguishing of spirits
allows the counsellor to discern if the counsellee is demon-
possessed.

6. *The Gift of Service*

The gift of service is mentioned in Romans 12:7. The
word 'service' comes from the Greek *diakonia* which can
also be translated as 'ministry'. Those endowed with the
gift of ministry enjoy serving the Lord in people-centred
service. They are never tired of ministering to others even
in the late hours of the night.

We know of doctors, for example, with such a gift. We
have been deeply inspired and touched by the Christian
spirit and dedication of some of the Christian doctors we
know. We have observed with thanksgiving the willingness with which they respond to the call of ailing patients
even in the small hours of the morning.

7. *The Gift of Exhortation*

The gift of exhortation is found in Romans 12:8. The word
'exhort' comes from the Greek *parakaleo* which also
means 'comfort'. The gift of exhortation, as such, is also
the gift of comfort. It is the ability to communicate the
comfort of the Lord through our very presence. It is the
special power conferred by the Spirit to bring the peace of
God into the lives of hurting people. It is a gift that all
Christian counsellors should seek.

The spiritual gifts as mentioned above aid the counsellor in his work of counselling. It is his right to seek these gifts that the Lord has made available to His people. Let us ask of the Lord, believing that we will receive, so that many others may be blessed.

Chapter 11

A Life Practice

God calls us to comfort His People so that we too can be comforted. If we are to be channels of God's Love and Comfort to others we cannot but be ourselves also open to the comfort of God. Hence God in His Wisdom, tells us to comfort others so that we may be part of His wonderful plan.

When we first met Maureen, she was a quiet and very withdrawn person. Her husband is a successful and accomplished person and Maureen has always felt inadequate. She was extremely sensitive and would be deeply hurt by what others said about her. She would cry so often that her husband would be exasperated and at a loss as to how to relate to her. She would also talk incessantly to her husband when he came home from work as an outlet for her pent-up emotions. This caused a strain on their marriage relationship. However, when Maureen came with her husband for training in Christian counselling, she discovered that she could identify with the ministry and began to avail herself for training and exposure. Her attitudes began to change as she met with persons who were under greater affliction than she was. Maureen and her husband decided to also request marriage counselling to sort out their own tangles. Meanwhile, Maureen had been ministering to her sister who suffered from depression. As part of the ministry team, and being the one closest to her sister, she played a key role in helping her sister out of her depression. This experience changed Maureen's entire outlook and life. She began to listen to her children and her husband for the first time in her life and stopped focusing on her own sense of inadequacy. Her husband and children found support in her and she experienced the fulfilment she had longed for. Maureen commented, 'If I had known that helping others was a way of helping myself, I could have done it much earlier in life because since my childhood I've wanted to be of help to others.'

As we give of ourselves to others in obedience to Christ, we learn the lessons of love that Jesus taught. Let us therefore take up the challenge to perfect ourselves in the Ministry of Comforting by learning what it means in our own personal lives to:

Draw Comfort from God,
Develop Readiness to Administer God's Comfort,
Develop a Ministry Lifestyle.

Draw Comfort From God

As we present our lives to God in a ministry to others, there will be times when Satan's attacks on us can threaten to overwhelm. A dear Christian lady Mrs Chan once told me (Shirley) of how restless and frustrated she became and how she hated herself for being the way she was. This loving lady had for many years used her cooking talent to minister regularly and sometimes weekly to those who were helpless because of old age or illness. She would cook for many charity fairs and for gatherings of the family and friends. However, she found herself lately losing the joys of her work as younger and more able cooks emerged in her fellowship circle. She knew it was really silly of her to resent the praises and compliments that used to be showered on her, now given to others. She spoke of how, despite her good intentions of not overreacting emotionally to the success of others, she would be very envious even of her own daughters and daughters-in-law. The tension of having to measure up and to compete with others was taking its toll on her. She got very depressed one day when a large portion of what she cooked was not eaten by her family. She threw a tantrum and almost hurt her grandchild. In the course of counselling, she began to recall her sense of rejection in her childhood and later on in adult life when she was deprived of tertiary education so that her brother could be sent to the university. She sought comfort from the Lord to soothe the pains of a lifetime of striving. She allowed the Lord to touch the very sensitive and closely guarded areas in her life and she was released to serve with joy and gladness in her heart.

Learning to draw comfort from God at every point of our lives is a maturing process for all of us. We can turn to the Lord directly or reach out for help from a compassionate friend. As we minister, the best of us become tired, worn-out and burnt out. When that happens, we lose our effectiveness as God's channel of blessing. Some of us may feel negative and discouraged at various points in life even though nothing seems to be outwardly wrong.

Effective Ministry

Mr Tan shared with us about a time of dryness he experienced when he felt very negative about his business ventures, his family and his health. 'This is not me,' he explained to us, 'I've always been cheerful and positive. I just don't know what has come over me.' Mrs Tan, his wife, has also been feeling unhappy over her husband's withdrawal for the last year or so. She felt his displeasure with her and was determined to help him get out of his depression. However, the more she tried, the more hurt she became as he not only rejected her help but refused to talk to her. The Tans have always been an exemplary Christian couple and the intensity of their recent misunderstanding made them negative and disillusioned. Mrs Tan came to us for prayer and counsel and wondered why she had not been able to minister to her husband in his need. 'I've tried to get him to talk about his problem but he just stubbornly refused to say a word. You know, I could talk for hours and still he wouldn't say a word! It's as if he has erected a wall between us. I told him how I felt about his shutting me out when all I wanted to do was to help and he would say he was sorry ... but what's the use? ... he still refuses to talk about it and when I cry and say we've got to pray about it, he would become very rude and say that I use my prayer to complain about him. I'm really discouraged to know that he can think this way about me!'

The problem the Tans have been going through is a common one. Christian couples experience this kind of 'impasse' to various degrees. Both the Tans are God-fearing Christians and love each other. Why have their attempts to minister to each other failed? We asked Mr Tan if he had tried to draw comfort from the Lord during these trying times. He said he tried to do that but found it difficult to shake off that sense of hopelessness and defeat. Clearly he needed help. Mrs Tan chipped in to say that she had known that all along and therefore had been trying to minister to him by making him talk to her about it. 'He just wouldn't allow me to minister the Lord's Comfort to him!' she complained. We began to help Mrs Tan to see that she has interpreted her husband's behaviour towards her as a personal attack on her, and she has become bitter towards him. How could she be of help in her disturbed state?

Mrs Tan then confessed that she had been distressed and troubled in her spirit and admitted her fears as for the first time in her life, she doubted her husband's love for her. 'If he loves me, why does he snap at me when I have only been trying to help?' Mrs Tan was made to recognise that her husband was really going through a tough patch and that she was in no position to help until she had herself found the Comfort of the Lord in her situation. As Mrs Tan drew close to the Lord, she began to exude to her husband the love of the Lord. Today, the Tans have an effective team ministry as they serve the Lord together.

To minister effectively, we need to draw true comfort and refreshment from God. As we turn to the Lord for comfort, honestly confessing our inadequacies and predicament, He refreshes us and gives us a new sense of purpose. In administering God's love to others, we need first to fill our hearts and minds with the love and comfort of the Lord and then simply allow the abundance of His comfort to flow through us. God can use us, but we must be open channels to allow the flow of His love to take place.

A lady who was abandoned by her husband and lost a large portion of her estate requested prayers and counselling to help her through her crisis. A few of us ministered with her and being a non-Christian, she was curious as to how we would react if we were in her situation. We empathised with her and said we would be very deeply hurt too but we have Jesus who can minister to our hearts and give us His comfort and joy in our sorrow. When she discovered that amongst us was a dear lady who had also been abandoned by her husband but was still full of love and prayers for him, she was very touched. She said to us, 'I've always wondered why you have that glow, that radiance on your faces. Now I know it's because you've got Jesus.'

It is important for us to allow the glow and radiance of the Lord's love to shine through our lives and countenances as we minister for Him. Often this transparency in us speaks much louder than anything we can say. Therefore let us take up the challenge to minister God's comfort to others by first drawing upon it for ourselves and for our own happy living.

Develop Readiness

'I really want to make my life count for Jesus. You see, I have always had a desire to help others. In fact, I get a lot of joy out of helping. The trouble is that as I look back at the last 50 years of my life, I can't really say I have done much. I somehow get so busy with my own affairs and...'

Isn't this how Christians often feel about reaching out to others? There is often the desire and even intention to do so but limitations of time and demands of life often crowd out our good intentions.

A Christian lady who had deep hurts from early childhood, told us of how nobody ever had time for her. As a child she was abandoned by her father, and her mother worked at a food-centre all day long to support the family. For as long as she could remember, she had been left either alone in the house or with the next door neighbours from dawn to nightfall. Nobody bothered about little Mary (we'll refer to her by this name). She grew up self-reliant and was in fact quite a leader. However, the fact that nobody ever had time for her was reinforced in her life. She tried to escape this painful thought by doing things for others instead of expecting anything from anyone. On the outside she seemed to be so strong and sure in her faith until her repressed feelings began to take control and she became incoherent and depressed. In the counselling sessions, one particular incident was repeatedly brought up – an incident that reinforced her underlying fear that nobody had time for her. She told of how she had stood outside a public building for hours, weeping, dazed and forlorn and there were people passing by but not one stopped to see if she needed help. This incident triggered off the deep sense of rejection she had been harbouring. She kept asking the question, 'Why doesn't somebody care?'

Our lifestyle in a fast urbanising society can breed an increased sense of loneliness and despair in some people. We find ourselves treasuring our much needed privacy in the face of a hectic work schedule. It often seems like too much trouble to stop and help one another in the journey of life. Perhaps they don't want to be helped and anyway, how much can I do? Satan has in his subtle way caused many to believe in untruths such as: 'It's no use for us to try to help others. It will only make matters worse for everyone concerned.' Satan's favourite line to discourage us and cause us to be negative is, 'You shouldn't be helping others. You're not good enough yet!'

When we assess this thinking against Scripture, we find that there is no truth in this kind of negative thinking at all. We are not told in Scripture that we are to be near perfect before we can express our care for others. In fact we are told in Scripture not to be preoccupied with thoughts about ourselves and indulge in *'empty conceit'*, but in humility to look to the needs of others (Philippians 2:3, 4).

Adopting this attitude of humility as exemplified in Christ (Philippians 2:5), we can develop a life practice of service to others wherever we are. We can begin by developing a readiness to help. Haven't we often been somewhat regretful on hindsight that we have missed an opportunity to be of help to someone because of our reticence and inexperience? Lee Mei recounted how she felt a deep sense of rejection when her mother had a heart attack suddenly one night. She recalled the trauma she experienced and the frenzy she was in. In desperation for help, she had knocked on the doors of her neighbours and called her friends on the telephone, all to no avail. Somehow, her friends and neighbours didn't seem to know what to do or didn't seem to want to be involved. Lee Mei shared with me (Shirley) how she felt when she saw her mother gasping her last breath as she held her in her arms. The feelings of anguish turned to bitterness as she wondered why God was not there, why no one was around. It wasn't anyone's fault as her mother had a massive heart attack but she couldn't help but wish that some of her friends and neighbours had been more ready to help.

A readiness to help others has to be developed. Very often, we find ourselves inhibited by our own uncertainties and find that we fail to respond in offering comfort when we are called upon to. We were driving along a quiet side road late one night when the engine of our car stalled and it refused to start again. 'We should have changed that old battery!' we muttered under our breath. We decided that one of us would push and the other steer the car. A group of four men walked by and we felt hopeful. They walked past, busy chatting. As we pushed and puffed, we approached a bus-stop. Oh good! Some more people in sight! Well-dressed youngsters, probably going to a late party. Surely they'll help! We heaved the car right past their staring eyes and not a soul stirred. 'We should ask someone, not just wait for offers of help,' we told ourselves. A uniformed watchman was walking to his motorcycle. We asked him if he could help. His body language exuded a message of resignation and reluctance but he helped push the car. At the first bend of the road, we turned around and found that he had disappeared. We were beginning to lose some of our faith in humanity when a group of tourists emerging from a hotel shouted in true holiday spirit, 'Need any help?'

As we drove the car on our way home, we mused over why there was that lethargy that prevents people from extending a helping hand. We were sure the people we saw were not all nasty people. Some of them looked nice. A lack of readiness, a pre-occupation, and a fear of being involved could be some of the reasons. This lack of readiness can often cause disillusionment and bitterness to those who need to depend on the goodwill of others at various points of their lives. Of course we should not be idealistic and think we can help eliminate all suffering from the world but we should at least be able to say that we are trying to do our part in developing a readiness to help and fight free of the tendency to look inward and live a life of self-centredness. Scripture reminds us of the need to move away from self-centredness by daily denying ourselves, by daily taking up the cross and following Jesus.

The Bible tells us explicitly to consider not only our own matters but to care for others as well (Philippians 2:4). Jesus Himself sets down for us the pattern for caring for those in need in the parable of the Good Samaritan (Luke 10:30–37). It is obviously a lesson for us to note that we are not to be like the Levite or the Priest who turned away from someone in need and walked another way. Our Lord is a God of love and if we have personally been touched by His love, we can continue to experience the same love by exercising it in loving ministry to others, especially the least amongst us. Offering Christ's love through our loving ministry to others, especially the least amongst us, must be our life's goal. Caring for those who are in need is important because it demonstrates the very love of Christ, the 'agape' love that reaches out to the unlovely. The 'agape' flow must be initiated before we can experience that growth and maturity that is in Christ.

A Positive Compassion

In the story of The Good Samaritan, Jesus illustrates to us the concept of positive compassion which results in constructive assistance to those in need. We read in verse 33 of Luke, chapter 10, that the Good Samaritan **felt compassion** when he saw the distressed man by the wayside and we read on in verse 34 that he *'bandaged up his wounds, pouring oil and wine on them; and he put him on his own beast, and brought him to an inn, and took care of him'*. Jesus reminds us in this parable that the true test of our love for God is our manifestation of love to others. When we have compassion for others, our response to their need is spontaneous and positive.

We can assume that the Good Samaritan was an ordinary person, a mere passer-by who may not have been a specialist in people-helping. His expression of care and concern for the man in need was the example Jesus used in defining a loving neighbourliness and a readiness to minister. The Levite and the Priest are clear examples of people who are not willing to exercise positive compassion. What is taught in this parable is that whether clergy or laity, the challenge to us is the same. The challenge is to develop a readiness to identify with the needs of others to the extent of rendering whatever help we are capable of mustering at any point of time.

What is Jesus saying to us about our own response to persons in need who come our way? What does it mean for us to have positive compassion? We notice that the Good Samaritan did immediately whatever he could for the man as a result of his compassion for him. We, too, are sometimes called upon to do what we can as a short-term measure of help for the distressed. Turning away a person with genuine need is not a loving act.

Notice also that the Good Samaritan seemed to know exactly what to do for the distressed man. He was not too shocked to help or too confused to be of much help. It seems to us that the Good Samaritan epitomises a Christian who is uninhibited and is well-prepared to do whatever he can to bring comfort to the distressed.

Mr and Mrs Joseph rang their fellowship group members for help when their baby became violently ill and was sent to the hospital. Their Christian friends called us to ask what they should do. The prayer chain had already been activated, and as one of the members went with the couple to the hospital the others stayed at home to mind the other children. We rushed to the home of the Josephs to find that another child had also been taken ill and it was certainly good for the Josephs to have caring friends who tended to the other children while they were at the hospital. It blessed our hearts to see the positive compassion of God's people in action. It is possible to develop a readiness to help.

A Giving of our Resources and Time

The story of the Good Samaritan that Jesus told holds useful guidelines for us in how we can be ready to involve ourselves in meaningful ways in the lives of persons in distress.

The Good Samaritan gave both his resources and time. We read of how he not only personally attended to the wounds of the distressed man but also put him on his donkey and brought him to an inn, paying in advance two days' wages for his stay. In today's context, the story would be interpreted as including the transporting of the man in a car to a fairly good hotel. Surely the lesson for us here is that we need to give of our money and resources to others in need as an expression of our love for God.

Apart from resources, we need to set aside time to minister to needs. It is often the experience of Christians that God allows us to encounter persons in situations of need. As we look at these occasions as opportunities for ministering the love of Christ, we will find a deep joy in service that strengthens our faith. If we choose to look negatively at these encounters as infringements of our time and privacy, we miss the blessing of being used as channels of God's peace to others. If we offer the love of Christ through positive involvement and care, we receive the joy of serving Christ Himself. Didn't Jesus say in Matthew 25:40 that if we have ministered to the least of our brethren, we have ministered to Christ Himself? So, let us together attempt to work out the scriptural directives for Christian care and counselling so that we can be effective parents, mentors, teachers, leaders and Christian friends.

A Link-up With Others

The Good Samaritan delegated the care of the distressed man to the innkeeper. This is an example of the need to sometimes link up with others so as to minister holistically to persons in need. There is no doubt that it is the Christian's call to familiarize himself with the support systems existing within the church and the community so that persons who come to him or her for help can be linked to those able to meet specific aspects of the distressed person's needs.

Jenny has always treasured her privacy and she has lived happily alone in her little house all her life. Lately however, she has been getting weaker and she suffers from gout and a weak heart. A Christian neighbour has been visiting her daily and bringing her food on days when she felt unwell and could not cook for herself. Jenny recounted how one day as she was watering the plants along her long driveway she felt a pain in her chest and collapsed. She called out for help but no one could hear her as her neighbours were far away. Her Christian neighbour had gone away for a holiday and as she lay helpless on the driveway, she realised that no one would discover her plight. Fortunately for Jenny, her Christian neighbour had in fact left word with the pastor that Jenny might need some overseeing while she was away. When the pastor called on Jenny, he found her helpless along the driveway and immediately sent her to hospital. Jenny explained that she had been helpless on the driveway for the last eight hours thinking of what would happen to her if nobody came along soon enough. She was thankful for the wisdom of her neighbour.

Developing a Ministry Lifestyle

We have noticed the Good Samaritan as an experienced people-helper. From the spontaneous and aptness of the support and help he gave, the Good Samaritan seemed to know exactly what to do. The Good Samaritan was not only compassionate and willing to help but he was also competent in helping. We too can cultivate competence in ministering God's Comfort to others and acquire a sense of what can be done and how we can best help others in need. As we avail ourselves of the practice of drawing comfort from God and in turn extending it to others, ministering becomes a lifestyle for us. Whether we are involved in formal or informal situations of Christian counselling, we can offer God's comfort through the following practices.

A Practice Of Listening

Jane's mother is a warmhearted lady who loves her daughter dearly. As an only child, Jane lived in the shadow of her doting mother. Jane grew up to be timid and suffered from a deep sense of inferiority as her mother is a very dominant and strong-willed person. Her mother made all decisions for her and took good care of her every need. At 29, Jane had never felt confident enough to live her own life and make her own decisions. Jane first came to see me (Shirley) because she had lapses in her memory and could not concentrate on her work as a clerical officer. She had not been able to keep a job for more than a few months at a time and could not relate to her colleagues who she thinks are against her. Jane's main problem was her mother. She could not relate to her mother. Jane felt that her mother made demands on her and would not listen to what she had to say. She would cry bitterly every time she spoke about her mother and once she cried out, 'Why can't she just listen to me for once? You know, Mrs Lim, only last week, when I bought a golden brooch for myself, she nagged at me to return the brooch for a golden ring instead. When I told her I needed a brooch and not a ring, she simply took the brooch herself and went down to the jewellery shop to have it changed! How could she do a thing like that? And all I could do was stare at her! I know it is a bad thing to say this, but I really hate my mother!'

If only Jane's mother would listen to her! Her mother had showered her with a doting kind of love and wanted to provide her with all that she needed without allowing her a chance to be herself and be heard. Jane became very depressed and was suicidal. When Jane's mother was helped to understand her daughter and began to learn to listen to what she was saying, Jane also became more receptive to help, and began pouring out her inner fears and insecurities. Jane slowly learned to accept the reality of Christ's love in her life and was released from her hurts as she forgave her mother.

Empathetic listening is a powerful assurance of love and acceptance. It assures the distressed that, while we do not condone any wrongdoing that they may have indulged in, there is an understanding of the strife and hurt that is experienced. The distressed find a great consolation in someone who listens empathetically because very often, they find that no one seems to understand them and the more upsetting problem is that they can't even understand themselves. The empathetic listener enables the distressed the opportunity to talk and work out his own uncertainties.

1. Empathy

It is often difficult for us to understand the feelings of others, but when we do, we are able to establish an emotional link that will enable our counsellees to open up to us. The practice of empathy is God's gift to us through our Lord Jesus Christ. Jesus, Who though He is God, took the form of man and walked the way we have walked so that He can have perfect empathy with us. He knows from first-hand experience what it means to be hurt and humiliated, rejected and falsely accused. Jesus also suffered physical torment and pain to the point of death for our sakes. He understands us in our pain.

The Christian counsellor in this ministry of listening is an ambassador of Christ to the counsellee and ministers relief and comfort in His Name. The counsellee will then realise that the empathy shown is an acceptance of the legitimacy of the counsellee's feelings, though not condoning the sins.

A Christian lady once described to me how she has over

the years been suffering from pains in the stomach and how she has kept it from even her family members as she did not want them to be unduly worried about her. She had been brought up in the belief that ladies should be discreet and not bother others with their personal problems. As a child, her father would insist that girls were to keep to themselves and they were not even allowed to have meals at the main table with the men in the family. So used was she to being relegated to a position of non-importance that when her husband and children insisted on knowing how she felt, she became ridden with a deep sense of guilt that she was a burden to the family. She refused to admit to sharp pains she felt in her body even though she collapsed often from the pains. Her withdrawal frustrated the family and she lived many years in a state of emotional estrangement from her loved ones. 'The problem with mum,' her eldest daughter said, 'is that she almost stubbornly props herself up to look well even if she felt poorly. I've never seen her cry before – just that mournful and cross look! – We just cannot reach her!'

As I (Shirley) spoke to this lady, I understood what her daughter meant. Mrs Wong rambled on about how important it is for a woman to be strong and self-reliant. She recounted to me the 'good old days', laughing about the discrimination against women and recalling how strong and enduring women in the past were. 'Do you know that I've never breathed a word of complaint even when I had ulcers in my stomach? Women nowadays, groan at the slightest headache!' she mused.

Although Mrs Wong spoke cheerfully, I could sense her rejection and remorse and was surprised that she looked happy and unaffected by the fact that she had to suffer in silence. I reached out to her and said, 'Mrs Wong, from what you have said, you must have gone through a great deal of pain. I can understand it if you feel miserable having to bear it all in silence like that.' At my words, she burst out in tears for the first time since we talked and said, 'Mrs Lim, you're quite right. I'm not really as happy and strong as I look. It's just that I never thought anyone would understand. They'll just think that I am weak and complaining.' With that release, Mrs Wong was able to speak for the first time about events that hurt her, without having to put on a show of courage. She was able to face her fears and see how she had allowed them to affect her relationships with her loved ones.

Listening is an absorbing involvement. We can listen not only to what is being said but also to what is being felt. Underlying the utterances are attitudes, intentions and emotions that are as important if not more important than what is being said in words. We need to ask God for clarity of mind and spirit when we listen to someone. Effective listening is not a self-centred but other-centred activity. This is because we must never allow pre-conceived perceptions and views to cloud our listening. It is so easy to project our own thoughts on to others when we listen only selectively to what is being said and jump to premature conclusions. We will not be able to help others if we hear only what we want to hear.

2. *Clarifying and Responding*

It is useful to counter-check with our counsellee our inter-pretation of what is being said and felt. Clarifications are useful because they allow time for fuller understanding of the problem and situation. Even good listeners may forget to counter-check on impressions simply because they assume they have understood. We need to remember that the aim of the counselling encounter is for the counsellee to receive help and not to prove the counsellor's abilities. Hence it is always useful to clarify what the counsellee has said, and be ready to retract if the counsellee does not agree with our reading of his situation. There is no point entering an argument with the counsellee on issues raised as he or she will certainly not be helped to understand the situation even if the counsellor wins the argument. Paul's words in the Book of Colossians are relevant to us here, *'Let your conversation be always full of grace, seasoned with salt, so that you may know how to answer everyone'* (Colossians 4:6).

A Christian counsellor in one of our training sessions said to us, 'I thought that I wouldn't make a good counsellor because I'm by nature direct and cutting in my remarks, but I was determined to allow the Lord to bridle my tongue when you shared this verse (Colossians 4:6) with me. Now, I find that I can be patient and kind. You see, it's love in my heart that does it. When my heart goes out in compassion for my counsellee, I just don't want to hurt him because I think he's hurt enough already to have to come to me!'

A Christian counsellor once brought her counsellee to meet with me (Shirley). The counsellee had recently gone through the traumatic experience of losing her entire family in a road accident. As she recounted the event of the fatal car-ride toward a holiday resort and how it all happened so quickly, she broke into sobs of pain and despair. Both the Christian counsellor and I wept with the counsellee as we could not control the tears that flowed. The counsellee looked up and when she saw our tears, she said, 'I really don't know how to thank both of you because I just feel so much love amongst you – you don't even know me and yet you're weeping with me. It's so comforting for me to know that I have friends like you and I know there must be something in what you are saying about Jesus being able to comfort me. Can I come and join you in your church service on Sunday?'

After the counsellee left, and the Christian counsellor and I had time together to discuss the preceding session, the Christian counsellor asked, 'Do you think it was wrong of us to weep just now? You know, some counsellors say we shouldn't be emotionally involved with the counsellee if we are to be of help.' This is often the question asked when we look at the practice of counselling from a theoretical standpoint. It is true that we should guard against projecting our personal emotions in a counselling situation and should remain as objective as possible but this does not mean that we become clinical and detached. We believe that whilst it is important for us not to allow an emotional response to influence our judgement, it is just as important to be able to feel with the counsellee to have an accurate assessment of the situation. We should not be afraid of exercising empathy. Indeed, we should always attempt to empathise because we can then be an open channel of blessing to the counsellee and enable the breaking down of barriers that may have been erected. We certainly need to minister to others as human beings with feelings rather than superficially as persons playing the role of someone who has the answers. Indeed, very often we do not have the answers. We are simply pointing the way to the One who is the answer. Jesus Himself empathised with Mary and Martha over the death of Lazarus to the point of Himself weeping. Empathy is an expression of the Love of God.

3. Confidentiality

Christian counselling gives counsellees the privilege of access to someone they can confide in. Christian counsellors will often experience counselling encounters during which counsellees come unprepared to disclose much of themselves. But as the counsellor listens empathetically, the counsellee begins to pour out unreservedly from the heart things he had never meant to share. This is why confidentiality should be strictly observed so that a relationship of trust can be maintained.

As openness and honesty are essential to reach the core issues in the counsellee's situation, there must be strict confidentiality. Confidence and trust in the Christian counsellor is of paramount importance. A person in need approaches a Christian counsellor usually out of a pressing need for support and direction. The counsellor needs to uphold that trust and confidence. As the ministry of probing and empathetic listening goes on, there will usually be a free flow in the sharing of pains, hurts and needs. Whilst there is often a sense of relief for the counsellee, there is sometimes a fear of being exposed. The counsellee therefore must be assured of understanding and confidentiality. Where there is a need to disclose facts or feelings to other persons, it is often useful to discuss with the counsellee the content and the extent of the disclosure. In such cases, the consent of the counsellee must be sought.

An Agape Flow

The basic and underlying motivation in Christian counselling is Christ's love. It is not so much our love for Christ, as our love is often fluctuating and inconsistent, but rather Christ's love for us that moves and enables us to love others. In 1 John 4:10–11, we are reminded that, '*In this is love, not that we love God, but that He loved us and sent His Son to be the propitiation for our sins. Beloved, if God so loved us, we also ought to love one another.*'

There is great joy as we return to Him something of His great love for us through serving the least among us. We know of many who, having experienced the love of God through the supportive hand of a compassionate counsellor would themselves reach out to others in need to tell of what God can do. Being a part of the flow of God's love into the lives of troubled souls is a joy that is immeasurable. God can so touch the lives of persons who are depressed, negative and despondent, that where there has been no real hope and love there is now hope and love in such abundance that it has to be shared and given out!

I remember a very long-drawn ministry with a highly depressed lady who was continually under medical care. Whenever there were signs of some improvement, something would happen to bring her spirits down again. There was this continual struggle at the brink of suicide and regret. At one point of the ministry, the Lord touched her attitudes and confirmed in her spirit His love for her. She was jubilant and said that she felt released and received a new and positive outlook. She called one day and said, 'Mrs Lim, I've got this friend whom I met when we were in the hospital, and I told her of how wonderful Jesus has been to me, and she wants to receive Jesus as well. Can she come and see you? I've shared with her a little but I think I need help with her ... can you help me help her?'

There have been times when I wondered if these exhilarating moments were just bubble experiences that would soon burst and leave her more depressed than ever. What caused me to marvel at the miracle of God's work in the lives of many is that the bubbles did not burst as they weren't just fleeting experiences. God has done such a complete work in the lives of many who were once under the power of the evil one. Today, their newfound lives with Christ reflect a new beauty. The wonder of it is that for many of them, the obsessions of the past have never come back and they stand as living witnesses of the goodness of the Lord.

The power of God's love can lift up the fallen. However, there are times when the counsellees' blatant defiance of God's laws can be heartbreaking for the counsellor who may find it increasingly difficult to minister. It can be very difficult to remain objective and maintain compassion for the counsellee whilst admonishing him for his sin. In these situations, the counsellor must be ready to handle his/her own emotions and refrain from reacting personally in anger or frustration to the extent of giving up being a helper altogether. We need constantly to examine our spirits to ensure that we have honestly maintained compassion for the person in need. In fact the heartache we may feel over counsellees who seem to choose the path of sin is nothing compared to the pains our Lord suffered as He was bruised for our iniquities. Hence the goal of Christian counselling is to offer compassion by the power of the Holy Spirit that the love of Christ may be seen.

A Practice Of Discerning

As the Christian counsellor listens and empathises with the counsellee, the counsellor also needs to be at one with God and sensitive to the promptings of the Holy Spirit who directs our ministry. The Christian counsellor stands as an ambassador of Christ extending His Love, His Grace and His Truth. Needless to say the counsellor must not harbour any known sin in his/her own life, but come as a channel of blessing cleansed by the Blood of Christ. Should the counsellor be conscious of known sin or emotional disturbance in his life, there is a need for personal confession before the Lord, followed by unconditional obedience to His Word. Needless to say, the blind cannot lead the blind and the Christian counsellor will want to be totally honest with God and rely completely on the leading of the Holy Spirit. Accordingly, the Christian counsellor is an open channel through which the love and direction of the Lord can flow to the counsellee. This constant dependence on the Lord makes Christian counselling an act of obedience and submission to the Will of God and prevents an attitude of self-righteousness and pride which will quite quickly be detected by the counsellee and used by Satan to cause confusion. Hence the Christian counsellor must be a diligent student of the Word of God, be fervent in prayer and constantly abide in Christ, appropriating the infilling of the Holy Spirit. In this way, the Christian counsellor ministers through the empowerment of the Holy Spirit, in the name of Jesus. The Spirit's guidance will lead us to discern the physical, emotional, intellectual and spiritual needs of the counsellee as problems and concerns are shared.

Whilst the physical needs of food, shelter and clothing are real enough and should be attended to through the Social Concerns Ministries of the Church, the more fundamental needs that can be effectively dealt with in Christian counselling are more than just physical or material needs. A sense of **self-worth** for example is not necessarily directly related to the possession of wealth or talent or even personal achievement. We have spoken to many who though outwardly successful and exuding an air of confidence and poise, lament that deep within there is an emptiness and fear of total annulment or destruction. The fear of being a nobody has driven many to depression and others into feverish activity to perform up to standard.

The Gospel of Christ offers both security and significance to man. This makes Christian counselling not only meaningful, but also fruitful for the Christian, as he has a great gift to offer to the poor afflicted soul. The Gift of Christ's love is of immeasurable value to the tormented human soul which is often full of negative forces that threaten total darkness and hopelessness. The task of Christian counselling is therefore to discern the most immediate pains afflicting the counsellee and to minister the love of God, and the truth of His Word through listening, directing and a ministry of prayer.

Where a counsellee's need is physical, the Bible clearly asserts the responsibility of the Christian to assist in meeting this need through the provision of food, drink, shelter and clothing (Matthew 25). Where the immediate need is social as in the need for a visitor or a friend, the Christian's responsibility is to be that friend or to be a channel for contact with such a friend.

The practice of discernment therefore refers to the direction that the counsellor receives from the Lord over the basic and specific needs of the counsellee. The counsellor also discerns what forms of ministry would be helpful for the counsellee. In some situations, counsellees need only to be listened to empathetically and the very experience of pouring out hurt feelings to a compassionate counsellor would provide the release. The counsellor at other times simply provides *'encouragement in Christ'* (Philippians 2:1) through reassurance of God's constant care and protection as stated in His Word. Ushering the counsellee into the very presence of God through prayer is one of the most powerful moments in the counselling ministry as the Holy Spirit heals and ministers on our behalf.

However, there are situations that require specialised attention. The handling of marital problems, for example, is best done through marriage counselling with both partners present. The lay counsellor must discern the needs and refer the case to more experienced marriage counsellors if necessary. Where there are signs of mental disorder, referrals should be made to doctors and psychiatrists. It is possible for the church to find support from Christian doctors and psychiatrists who would work hand in hand with the church in the ministry of healing and wholeness. The integrative approach allows for this and we have seen the benefits of team ministries in the counselling of relational problems involving members of the family and loved ones. Lay counsellors should see the value of consulting their pastors, church leaders and other relevant professionals to form counselling teams if the counsellees consent.

Discerning the counsellee's need for 'lapse time' or time to be alone to work things out is also important. As lay Christian counsellors, we respond to individuals who approach us for support in times of need. We should never pester or hound a counsellee in aggressive pursuit because this will defeat the very purpose of a helping ministry.

A Practice Of Other-centredness

Paul in his letter to the Church in Philippi, wrote of the importance of looking to the interest of others and to esteem them higher than ourselves (Philippians 2:3). In the light of this, we need to take the risk of trusting, loving and respecting others if we are to be like Christ. Paul wrote in the same chapter in verses 6 to 11 of how we need to emulate Christ and humble ourselves as Christ did in *'taking the form of a bond-servant, ... He humbled Himself by becoming obedient to the point of death, even death on a cross'* (Philippians 2:7, 8). It is only in humbling ourselves and loving the way Christ did that we can inspire trust and confidence in those who come to us for Ministry.

The Christian counsellor must be willing to carry the cross of humility as he ministers. As he humbles himself, God will exalt him. Humility and exaltation marked the ministry of our Lord while on earth. Humility and exaltation will also be our experience as we obey God in presenting our lives to Him as a living sacrifice in the ministry of counselling. We need to reach a level of commitment when we can like Paul say, *'But even if I am being poured out as a drink offering upon the sacrifice and service of your faith, I rejoice and share my joy with you all.'* When we express this agape love to others they will see that it is indeed God who is at work in us *'both to will and to work for His good pleasure'* (Philippians 2:13). It is only in Christ and through Him that we are able to exercise a ministry of 'other-centredness'.

In the 'other-centred' approach, the counsellor views matters in relation to how they affect the counsellee and has his welfare at heart. In this way, the counsellor seeks to do that which is best for the counsellee. It is important for the counsellor to guard against pre-conceived thinking or premature conclusions. This puts the counsellee into a set mould without the counsellor fully understanding the concerns of the counsellee. Hence there is a need to probe and question for feelings and underlying concerns.

Effective questioning and listening will assist the counsellor as he ministers to the needs of the counsellee. However the counsellor must guard himself against probing out of personal curiosity. Hence, in probing, the counsellor should not digress from the intention of establishing the facts and attaining greater understanding of the counsellee's situation so as to promote the counsellee's self-understanding.

The practice of 'other-centredness' therefore involves a deliberate effort to understand the counsellee's predicament to the extent of being able to empathise with him or her. The concern flows from a deep compassion and considerations are made from the standpoint of what is best for the counsellee in the light of God's Word. As we minister in this way, the counselling encounters will be a blessing for the counsellee as well as the counsellor who will reap the joy of obedience to the Lord.

A Practice Of Directing

It has been a question of some controversy amongst counselling circles as to whether the counsellor should at all be directing or telling the counsellee what should be done. There is the theoretical consideration of the rights and responsibility of the counsellee as an individual to make his or her decisions and the important premise that the counsellor should not attempt to interfere with the decision-making mechanisms of life.

Whilst it is true that the counsellee should be encouraged to make personal decisions and bear the consequences of his or her choices, it is difficult in a church-based setting to promote an absolutely non-directive approach. The counsellee who seeks church-based counselling almost invariably expects the counsellor to offer scriptural principles and guidelines. If Christian counselling is seen as a means of acquainting an individual with the love of Christ by bringing him or her into the presence and awareness of Christ, then it is important to introduce the appropriate guidance as given in Scripture relevant to the situation at hand.

In searching Scripture for general direction in the practice of Christian counselling, we have learnt a great deal from the way Jesus Himself handled His encounters with different people. In these encounters, we see Jesus directing the enquirer's attention to various important concerns. It was important for Jesus to deal with the sinful condition of man. The understanding of man's sinful nature, the need for personal conviction of sin and the release that repentance brings, are important basic considerations. One of the goals of Christian counselling is to help counsellees identify needs and to direct them to Scriptural truths related to these needs. Where there is known sin, they can be helped to turn away from sin and its entrapments. The process of Christian counselling identifies areas of darkness through which Satan has wrought pain and torment. If anguish is part of the process of pruning and growth for the Christian and if no known sin or misconduct is evident, then the role of Christian counselling is to lend encouragement in the faith, directing toward a personal dependence on the Lord. In both cases, the direction is always towards the power of Christ to redeem and regenerate.

What better example can we follow than that of Jesus as He counselled those who came to Him? He directed them towards the general truths laid down in Scripture, towards the need to deal with specific areas of their lives, and towards the need to abandon a life of immorality into faith in Him. He gave them guidelines for living. To others who were evidently insincere enquirers or those not ready for direct guidance, Jesus used parables and allusions to give general guidance.

While it is generally not advisable for the counsellor to be directive in the sense of making decisions for the counsellee, a Christian counsellor needs to lay down general guidelines that will assist the counsellee in decision-making.

A lady who was anorexic was directed to Scripture to understand how deeply God loved her and that she could also learn to love herself. She had put herself on a strict diet of only a few pieces of salad every meal. She became thin and undernourished but still felt she was fat and overweight. With a great deal of compassion and understanding, she was helped to love herself and began to eat sensibly. The Word of God spoke to her of Christ's love and concern for her and she began to find new meaning in life. When she was eventually healed, she was able to help another anorexic teenager who was close to death from voluntary starvation.

Loving direction toward the truth of Christ releases persons from the bondage of sin into an experience of hope. The sharing of God's directions to counsellees enable them to see their predicaments in the light of Scripture and serves as a prelude to freedom and release.

A Process Of Growth

Whilst only some will receive a call to the ministry of counselling in a full-time capacity, all Christians are to be ready to play a supportive part, however small it may be. It may merely involve listening to a friend or colleague who needs to share a burden and then to bring them to the church for counselling. Whatever the level of involvement, a caring and outreaching stance is required of a Christian. The Bible tells us that it is by our love that others will know that we are His disciples (John 13:35). Hence Christian counselling is a task that involves all Christians.

As we involve ourselves with others in genuine concern for them and not out of personal interest or gain, the Holy Spirit uses us to effect change not only in the lives of those in need but also in our own lives as well and we grow in spiritual maturity. We learn what it means to love, to accept disappointment, to trust God and to depend on His Grace. We also learn a great deal about ourselves and the nature of man. Spiritual growth can be experienced through caring ministries.

In the daily run of life, the Christian finds himself approached by friends and loved ones for a listening ear and counsel. Wherever he goes, human needs abound and many would turn to the Christian who has the peace and joy of Christ for counsel and empathy. Christians in helping professions, particularly doctors, teachers, nurses, lawyers and those in leadership positions are often in strategic positions to minister God's love as many would come to them for help. Sometimes, friends and acquaintances turn to us for counsel in a moment of need. These are opportunities for us to extend God's love and participate in Christ's ministry of love. The more we learn to respond to the needs around us, the more likely will those in need approach us for help. As we practise a life of living for others, we find a special meaning for ourselves too. In Ephesians 4:11–13, Paul tells us that members of Christ's body need to exercise the gifts given to them so that *'the body of Christ may be built up ... until we all attain to the unity of the faith and of the knowledge of the Son of God, to a mature man, to the measure of the stature which belongs to the fulness of Christ.'*

As we open our hearts and lives to minister to others, we will certainly receive for ourselves a deep sense of gratification. The challenge for the Christian counsellor is to respond to the fullness of life in Christ not only for himself but also for others, especially those whose lives are so enveloped in darkness that there is indeed no light.

The church is often a place of refuge for the troubled and distressed. When it is known within the community that the church opens its doors of ministry to those in need, many would come out of a genuine need. Apart from the influx of those outside the church who may want to make use of the facilities of counselling and care that the church provides, there are always many within the membership of the church itself who will from time to time need special care. In a general way, our loved ones at home and those closest to us need our ministry of comfort and love as well.

The Christian can be trained to be part of a ministry network to help persons going through various forms of emotional pain. If he avails himself as a soldier in God's army, willing to be disciplined and trained for the battle, there is a victory over the influences of the Evil One that he can claim for himself and for those he ministers to.

Conclusion

Tidings of Comfort and Joy

As the pressures of life come our way, we will sometimes feel stretched and drained as we attempt to open ourselves and be a part of the lives of persons outside our family and fold. As we respond to God's call to a greater extension of Personal Ministries particularly at the lay level, there will be new bridges to cross and new heights to climb. Together with new heights of elation and victory will be new battles and hardship, as the difficulties and pains of ministry come our way. However, as we persist in obedience, even though we feel stretched in spirit and sinew, God will surely strengthen us and give us the victory in Him. The wonderful truth we have discovered is that at the end of that road of struggle in obedience, the reward will always be a joy beyond expression.

Indeed, Jesus had never meant to push us on to more work, more self-sacrifice, more giving to deprive us of life's joys. No! We know that Jesus wants us to give more because that is the only way in which Jesus can fulfil His Will to bless us beyond all that we can ask or think! Because Jesus loves us and wants to bless us richly, He calls us to a ministry for others.

Do you sense the call and feel the weight of that conviction? Are we willing to stretch that second mile for the Lord to touch someone personally with His comfort and joy? Let us pray that we will all say, 'Here we are, Lord, send us!'

We may be successful in our careers, we may have reached peaks in our professions, we may have brought up our families well, done good through societies, associations and friends, and we praise God for all that! However, what joy can surpass the knowledge that somewhere in a quiet, forgotten corner is a person who has seen the love of God, our Father, because you have personally brought those tidings of comfort and joy?

We have been deeply blessed in being a part of a continuous flow of God's comfort. We hold fond memories of God's grace and power, some of which we have attempted to share with you in this book. We pray that by so doing, you will be encouraged to continue trusting His comfort and love despite temporary setbacks that may come your way.

We would like to close the challenge in this book by recalling our precious memories of God's comforting grace on people like Trevor.

Trevor was a doctor and a man of many talents. For many years his wife Ruth had been praying that he would come to know the Lord personally. We too prayed with Ruth for a long while before we learned to see visibly God's answers to our prayers. As the years passed by, we finally saw Trevor coming to Church with Ruth. It was a miracle for us to see Trevor's scepticism turn to spiritual fervour and deep conviction.

Trevor contracted cancer of the nose and the pharynx. We remember praying for Trevor and with Trevor, that the Lord's comfort and peace would come upon him. God answered our prayers and touched Trevor in a special way. God's comfort and peace rested so firmly on Trevor that after his death, Ruth testified that Trevor had never complained or blamed God. Through his illness, Trevor wanted only to reach out to others with the message of God's love and comfort, and many were blessed. In

Ruth's testimony she said, 'I was devastated when Trevor's illness worsened and it was Trevor who remained strong in the Lord and comforted me!'

The message and challenge Trevor leaves with us is clear. We can be messengers of God's Comfort to others no matter what happens to us. Let us rejoice in His love and spread afar with confidence the message of God's Comfort. Let us remember that there is a crying need in the souls of men, women and children which only the Comfort of Christ can adequately meet, and that we are called to be a part of Christ's Mission of love to the world. As we respond, let us be comforted that victory has been promised by our God who reminds us in Proverbs 11:14 that *'where there is no guidance, the people fall. But in abundance of counsellors there is victory.'* Praise God for the promise of victory as together we seek to respond to His call.

> **'Comfort, O comfort My people.'**
> **says your God.**   (Isaiah 40:1)

Notes

Chapter 3

1. Bernard Thompson, *Good Samaritan Faith*, (Ventura: Regal Books, 1984), p. 13.
2. Howard Clinebell, *Basic Types of Pastoral Care and Counselling*, (Nashville: Abingdon Press, 1984), p. 395.
3. Gary R. Collins, *Christian Counselling*, (Waco: Word Books, 1980), p. 17.

Chapter 4

1. Words in parenthesis are ours.
2. William M. Greathouse, 'Body' in *Beacon Dictionary of Theology*, edited by Richard S. Taylor, (Kansas: Beacon Hill Press of Kansas City, 1983), p. 80.
3. Richard S. Taylor. 'Soul' in *Beacon Dictionary of Theology*, edited by Richard S. Taylor, (Kansas: Beacon Hill Press of Kansas City, 1983), p. 495.
4. Ibid.
5. Donald Guthrie, *New Testament Theology*, (Illinois: Inter-Varsity Press, 1981), p. 172.
6. Ibid. p. 173.
7. Robert Frost, *Set My Spirit Free*, (New Jersey: Logos International, 1973), p. 75.
8. Ibid.
9. Donald Guthrie, *New Testament Theology*, (Illinois: Inter-Varsity Press, 1981), p. 169.
10. Ibid.

Chapter 5

1. Gary R. Collins, *Christian Counselling*, (Waco: Word Books, 1980), p. 23.
2. Paul D. Meier, Frank B. Minirth, Frank Wichern, *Introduction To Psychology and Counselling*, (Grand Rapids: Baker Book House, 1982), p. 291–292.
3. William Backus, *Telling the Truth to Troubled People*, (Minneapolis: Bethany House Publishers, 1985), p. 19.

Chapter 6

1. John and Paula Sandford, *The Transformation of the Inner Man*, (Plainfield: Bridge Publishing, Inc.), p. 16.
2. Ibid. p. 17.

Chapter 8

1. W.E. Oesterley, 'The General Epistle of James', in *The Expositor's Greek Testament*, Volume IV, edited by W. Robertson Nicoll, (Grand Rapids: Wm B. Eerdmans Publishing Company, 1976 reprint), p. 473.

Chapter 10

1. The words in parenthesis are ours.

Comments

Dr John Garlock, *Christ For the Nations Institute Dallas, Texas, USA comments:*

'The Lims' work on counselling is a rare accomplishment in that it shows both the academic excellence of a fine researcher and also the tender, caring heart of a pastor. They present the problems – and the answers – of this vital ministry by a balanced combination of case histories, Bible references, and scientific principles. They are inspiring without being "preachy." They are sympathetic without being maudlin.

An outstanding (and perhaps unique) feature of the book is that it does not consider counselling to be an esoteric speciality to be reserved for the degreed professional. Rather it appeals to all

Christians to be sensitive and responsive to their family, friends and neighbours. Then, even more important, it gives them the principles to help them help others.

Because Rev. and Mrs Lim base their approach upon caring, rather than upon technique, their words have universal application. This is not a book of formulas, pat phrases, or easy answers with guaranteed results. It is thoughtful, deeply compassionate, and solidly supported; it is also very practical because it is loaded with useable suggestions for helping people in emotional pain.

Anyone involved in aiding those in trouble will be helped by *Comfort My People*. I recommend it.'

Bishop Emerito P. Nacpil, *The United Methodist Church, Philippines,* **comments:**

'Using the Christian understanding of salvation, biblical knowledge, and profound insights gained from counselling people in a specific cultural situation, Isaac and Shirley Lim have written a book of unusual sensitivity and compassion to people in trouble and of how the Gospel brings healing and comfort. As a result one who reads the book will himself be comforted by the Gospel. He will also be compelled to share that healing and comfort with others, and the book provides guidance for doing just that. Ministers and lay persons will find in this book a rich resource for Christian counselling.'

Dr John Haggai, *Founder, Haggai Institute for Advance Leadership Training, Atlanta, Georgia, USA comments:*

'*Comfort My People* is a book long overdue. I thank God Isaac and Shirley Lim paid the price to write it. Blessed be the objective; bringing people to Christ – for all their needs. This volume is thorough, solid, biblical.

I like the emphasis that the larger the church, the stronger the personal ministries must be.

Though the Lims are thoroughly trained, academically and theologically, this volume is no spin-off of ivory tower theorizing. It lays out the principles of counselling for laypersons, predicates them on the truths of God's Word, and illustrates them by case studies both biblical and contemporary.

This book is a valuable addition to the software of today's church.